The Treasury of Devotion:
Sant Charaṇdās's *Bhaktipadarth*

The Treasury of Devotion:
Sant Charaṇdās's *Bhaktipadarth*

Translated from Hindi
by
Peter Friedlander and Harry Aveling

Prestige Books International
Delhi : Sydney

Published by
Prestige Books International
New Delhi 110 060
email: prestigebooks@gmail.com

Associate Office
10, Folkard Street,
North Ryde, NSW 2113, Australia

ISBN: 978-93-82186-34-2

Printed in India

Contents

Introduction

The Treasury of Devotion belongs to the *Sant* school of Hinduism. Literally, the word *sant* derives from the Sanskrit *sat* ("truth," "reality") and suggests "one who knows the truth," "one who has experienced Ultimate Reality" (Schomer 1987, 2). Something more than that. The *sants* sang about what they had known. They were poet-mystics. As Osho Rajneesh has said:

> The sant is a festival. An enlightened consciousness manifests itself in many ways: someone creates the statues of Khajuraho, someone carves out the caves of Ajanta and Ellora, someone dances, someone composes songs, someone remains silent. But one thing is certain: if you look deeply into them, they are all expressions of great poetry, unprecedented poetry. What form that poetry takes, what color—that is another matter. Most often, the sages have sung. They have sung what they wanted to say; they have not just said what they wanted to say, they have sung it, hummed it, ecstatically. There is a difference between the two (Osho Rajneesh 2001, 8-9).

More precisely again: the *sants* were popular Marathi and Hindi language poets who wrote about loving devotion to the divine. Most commonly they described the divine as being beyond all forms (*nirguṇa*)—as Paramātman, Supreme Spirit. Jñāneśvar (1275-1296), Nāmdev (1270-1350), and Eknāth (1548-1600) are outstanding figures originating from Maharashtra; Kabīr (traditionally dated 1318-1518, Vaudeville 1974, 37), Nānak (1469-1539) and Dādu Dāyal (1544-1603) are famous names at the beginning of the *sant* tradition in Hindi. Charaṇdās (1703-1782) and Palṭū Sāhib (late eighteenth century) are among the last *sant* teachers in the Hindi language tradition and are not as widely known in the West as their predecessors.

In this Introduction, we would like to survey what is known about Charaṇdās's life and the movement he founded, then to describe briefly some of the major themes in the present work.

Charaṇdās

Because Charaṇdās lived in the eighteenth century of the Common Era, there are many easily available sources on his life and teachings. Some are in fact contemporary and were written by himself or his immediate disciples. The first is the *Jñānsvarodaya*, one of the works included in Charaṇdās's major collection *Bhaktisāgar*. The second is the highly guru-devotional *Sahajaprakās* (The Brightness of Simplicity, 1743), by Sahajo Bāī, which gives precise information in Ragas 7 and 8 on his date of birth, 1703, and, throughout, on the life of his community. The third, Rāmrūp's *Gurubhaktiprakās* (The Illumination of Devotion to the Guru) was composed in 1769, during Charaṇdās's lifetime, and is "oriented towards doctrinal matters" (Gold 1987: 67). A further major work is the *Līlā Sāgar* (The Sea of Divine Play) by Jogjīt, which is "longer and more anecdotal" than the *Gurubhaktiprakās,* and whose "Vaishnava predilections" are more obvious (Gold 1987: 69, 72).

There is also a tradition of the Mahants ('Abbots') of the Charaṇdāsī tradition composing lives of Charaṇdās. Among these are a verse version of the life published in 1968 by Gaṇgādās, the Mahant of the Sahajo Bāī branch of the tradition (Gaṇgādās 1968) and a prose version of the life published in 2000 by Ghanśyām Dās, the current Mahant of the same branch of the tradition (Dās 2000). Ghanśyām Dās has stated that his work was based on Jogjīt's *Līlā Sāgar*, Rāmrūp's *Guru Bhaktiprakaś* and Gaṅgādās's work and it therefore represents a contemporary description summing up what is known of Charaṇdās's life.

In the *Jñānsvarodaya*, Charaṇdās writes:

I was born in Dehra
and named Rañjīt.
Son of Muralīdhar

recognized as a Ḍhūsar by caste.
As a child
I came to Delhi.
In my wanderings I met Śukdev
Who gave me the name Charaṇdās. (Charaṇdās 2001: 125)

Dehra is near Alwar in Rajasthan. The *Ḍhūsar* are members of the *baniyar* merchant caste, although they also have some claims to an ambivalent Brahmin status. Rañjīt and his mother, Kuñjo Rānī, came to Delhi in order to be with her family, after the disappearance of his father, who vanished into the forest; the father may have suffered an accident or, alternatively, gone off to follow a group of wandering ascetics. As a child, Rañjīt claimed to have had an initial vision of the divine sage Śukdev, although his elders could not see what he saw (Dās 2000: 9). In Dehra and Delhi, Rañjīt received brief periods of religious instruction from both Pandits and Mullahs but these apparently made little impression on him, compared to his own personal experience:

The mullah called on him to read;
The *bhaktiraja* heard him and said nothing.
He kept on thinking in his mind:
I've read enough—no more! (Gold 1987: 73, from Jogjit, 48)

As a teenager, Rañjīt himself spent long periods meditating in the forest. At the age of nineteen, after three years of unsuccessful searching for a guru, he met Śukdev again at Sukra Tal, and was initiated into the ascetic life, possibly with the complete name of Śyām Charaṇ Dās (Das 2000), although Sahajo Bāī calls him Rām Charaṇdās (in Raga 39). The initiation was done in the traditional style, with a bath and a mark on the forehead, as well as the transmission of a mantra. Śukdev may have been "a faqir of high religious attainments," as W. Crooke (1896: 202) presents him; Charaṇdās, however, identified him with the perpetually youthful son of the divine sage Vyāsa who was reputed to have divided the *Vedas*, recited the *Mahābhārata*, and composed the *Purānas*, whom he had already met while still a child.

The newly initiated *sādhu* then spent a period of some fourteen years practising yoga and devotion in a cave in the wilderness outside Delhi. Rāmrūpjī describes Charaṇdās's practices as including Patanjali's eight-limbed yoga, *rāja* yoga, *bhakti* yoga and *sāṅkhya* yoga; as Gold notes, these descriptions mainly follow the *sant* vocabulary to do with meditation used by Charaṇdās himself, including *surat* and *nirat*, and the *anahad shabda* (Gold 1987: 72).

In 1738, Charaṇdās began accepting followers in what is now Old Delhi, and continued teaching there for the rest of his life, with occasional trips into the countryside. He gained immediate fame by predicting the invasion of Delhi by Nadir Shah of Persia six months before it happened; he recorded the future dates of the arrival and departure of the invader in writing and gave these to a Muslim noble, who eventually showed the note to Nadir Shah himself. His disciple-biographers state that Nadir Shah was impressed and summoned Charaṇdās, who, however, refused to come. Thrown into prison as possibly being a dangerous magician, Charaṇdās vanished and was arrested a second time at home the following day. Although he had been bound in chains, Charaṇdās then appeared to Nadir Shah as the latter was sleeping and gave him a kick in the head. Nadir Shah had Charaṇdās taken home in royal style and a few days later paid court to the holy man, saying, according to Jogjit:

> Know him as of the race of God
> And banish bigotry
> Whether he's a Hindu or a Turk
> He's still God's light.
> (Gold 1987: 74-75, 227, from Jogjīt, also Rāmrūpjī)

In the countryside, Charaṇdās was often the guest of local rulers and Rāmrūpjī's biography includes a chapter entitled "Shri Maharaj Ji Lives in Delhi Like a Prince" (Gold 1987: 67). His most important journey was that taken in mid-life to Vraj, where he had a vision of Kṛṣṇa, followed by a further vision of Śukdev. Approximately a quarter of Rāmrūpjī's biography is filled with scenes set in Vrindavan (Gold 1987: 80).

Charaṇdās died in 1782 (Chaturvedi: 1972). By then his followers were spread across Rajasthan and the Punjab, and well into the Gangetic plain. Although Juktānand was appointed his successor, a disciple of Rāmrūpjī, named Siddha Rām, filed a suit against the legitimacy of Juktānand's claim. After a month's deliberation, the judge resolved that the temple would go to neither man but to Sahajo Bāī instead. This too was disputed. Eventually, it was decided that all three figures should live in their own houses, not in the temple, and thus the leadership of the movement was divided between these disciples and their successors. The pattern continues to this day.

Charaṇdās's Written Works

Charaṇdās was a prolific author; around twenty works are attributed to him. Many of these works deal with devotional practices, particularly relating to the worship of Kṛṣṇa. Others comment on various *upanishads* and yogic practices. The dates provided below are those proposed by Śukla (1995: 132-61):

Naseketalīlā varṇan (The Description of Naciketas, ca. 1726), the story of the youth Naciketas and his debate with death, based on the *Brahmānanda Purāṇa* and originally derived from the *Kathā Upanishad.*

Jāgaran Mahātmaya (The Greatness of the Vigil, ca. 1767), on the greatness of keeping vigil on the night of the eleventh day of the lunar fortnight.

Dānlīlā (Alms Giving Drama, ca. 1767), an account of Kṛṣṇa's stealing butter from the gopis, together with discourses and events related to this story.

Makhancorilīlā (The Butter Stealing Drama, ca. 1767), a short appendix to the *Danlīlā,* which is based, like the previous work, on the *Bhāgavata Pūrāṇa*

Kālināthanlīlā (The Kaliya Serpent Drama, ca. 1767), a short account of Kṛṣṇa's battle with the serpent king Kāliya.

Matkilīlā (The Pitcher Drama, ca. 1767), a short work on Kṛṣṇa and the gopis.

Sridhar Brahmanlīlā (The Brahmin Sridhar Drama, ca. 1767), a short work on the plan of Kamsa, king of Mathura, to kill the infant Kṛṣṇa.

Kuruksetralīlā (The Kurukshetra Drama, ca. 1773), a large work describing a visit to the pilgrimage site of Kurukshetra by Kṛṣṇa and the gopis on the occasion of a solar eclipse.

Charaṇdās's main work is the *Bhaktisāgar* (The Ocean of Devotion), an anthology of diverse texts including those already mentioned and those described below. In it, he explains that he decided on the Monday of the full moon of the month of *Caitra*, VS 1781 (1734 CE), to write his teachings down. Having begun, he eventually wrote down some 15,000 verses but decided to communicate only 5,000 to his followers.

The *Bhaktisāgar* includes the following works:

Vrajacaritra (The Deeds in Vrindavan, CE 1740), an account of Kṛṣṇa and Radha's activities in Vrindavan, composed when Charaṇdās was about 37 years old.

Amarlok (Immortal World, 1755), another work about Radha and Kṛṣṇa, set in the heavenly realm.

Dharmajahāj (The Ship of Dharma, 1743), a dialogue between a disciple and his guru on the nature of devotion and the practice of image worship (*saguṇ bhakti*).

Aśtaṅgayogavarṇan (The Description of the Eight Limbs of Yoga, 1743-55), a further dialogue between the disciple and the guru on the elements of yoga.

Yogasandehsāgar (The Ocean of Doubts Concerning Yoga, 1751), a further dialogue on the details of yoga practices,

Jñānsvarodaya (Wisdom on the Arising of the Breath, before 1757), a popular treatise on divination with regard to where and when the breath arises in the body.

Pañcopanisad arthavanaveda bhāṣā (An Exposition of Five Upanishads and the *Atharva Veda*, 1758-1763), a commentary on five upanishads associated with the *Atharva Veda*: *Hamsanada, Sarva, Tattvayoga, Yogashikha,* and *Tejabindu.*

Bhaktipadarthavarṇan (Description of the Elements of Devotion, 1764-1769), a detailed account of the various elements of the path of devotion.

Manaviraktakarana gutka sār (The Essence of the Treatise on the Renunciation of the Mind, 1750), a treatise on devotion to the guru, based on the eleventh chapter of the *Bhagavad Gita.*

Brahmajñānasāgar (The Ocean of the Wisdom of Brahma, 1757-1761), *sant* teachings

Sabda (Verses, composed at various times prior to 1763), a collection of separate verses on a wide range of themes, including invocations, arati worship texts, morning prayers, verses of warning, etc.

Bhaktisāgar (The Ocean of Devotion), on the nature of devotion and yoga, which gives its name to the whole anthology and is the only work which bears a date, 1734 CE. This is perhaps the date of the commencement of writing of this text, not of its completion, which was possibly about 1763.

Traditional Hindi Sources on Charaṇdās

By the second half of the nineteenth century, printing was becoming commercially viable in North India and Charaṇdās's works were widely available in this form. The British Museum acted as a copyright deposit for the first editions of books published in India. Blumhardt's 1891 catalogue of works held in the Museum library includes copies of a version of Charaṇdās's story of Naciketas, published in Bombay in 1858, and an edition of the *Bhaktisāgar* published in Lucknow in 1889 (Blumhardt 1893: 32). The *Jñānsvarodaya* was also published in Lucknow in 1874, as well as a further edition of the *Bhaktisāgar* in 1895 (Stark 2007: 396). Grierson (1910: 368) lists print editions of the *Jñānsvarodaya* from Delhi from 1876; the *Sandehasāgar, Dharamajāhaj, the Brahmavidyāsāgar* and, again, the *Nasiketopakhyana,* from Bombay in 1882; a third edition of the *Bhaktisāgar,* together with sixteen minor texts, Lucknow 1903, as well as in Bombay 1903; and the *Bānīs*, Allahabad 1903. A number of presses were active in promoting his works, and Blumhardt's 1913 supplement to his earlier catalogue includes titles published by presses in Bombay, Allahabad, Moradabad and Lahore.

Some of the earliest detailed sources in Hindi on Charaṇdās's life and his followers are to be found in prefaces to editions of his works from the Śrīveṅkateśvār Press. In the introduction to the *Bhaktisāgarādi* (2001), first published in Mumbai around 1900, Khemrāj Śrīkṛṣṇadās establishes the authenticity of his edition by recounting that it was a corrected version of a manuscript obtained by a Charaṇdās follower Pandit Rāmśaraṇdās of Kanakhal (Haridwar) from his friend Śivdāyal, an advocate in the high court in Jaipur.

This influential edition of the *Bhaktisāgar* contains a short account of the life of Charaṇdās which must have been based on Charaṇdāsī order traditions of its time. According to this tradition, he was born in 1703 CE in Dehra in Alwar. Eight generations before this, Charaṇdās's ancestor Śobhādās had pleased Kṛṣṇa with his devotion and was granted a boon that a partial incarnation of Kṛṣṇa would be born in his family for the liberation of living beings. Charaṇdās's father merged into the divine when the son was five. When he was 19, he had a vision of Śukdev at the place on the shore of the Ganges called Śuktāl, where Śukdev had recited the *Bhagavatpurāṇa* to King Parīkṣit. Charaṇdās then took initiation from him and went to Delhi and practised yoga and devotion for fourteen years. Following this, he went to Vrindavan and had a vision of Kṛṣṇā and then of Śukdev again. Following this he returned to Delhi and taught countless people about the nature of devotion. He became famous and performed many miracles, to the point that even Muhummad Shah, Emperor of Delhi, was his follower and gave him countless villages. The reason for this was that Charaṇdās was able to predict that Nadir Shah of Iran was going to attack Delhi six months before it took place. Finally he died in Delhi in 1782 at the age of 80.

The introduction to the Avadhsamacār Press edition of the *Bhaktisāgar* (1903) also contains a short introduction to the life of Charaṇdās, which must have been based on traditions then current in Lucknow, its place of publication. It is quite different from the account in the Śrīveṅkateśvār edition. According to this text, his father's name was Murlidhār and his own birth name was Rañjītsiṅgh; he was born into the *ḍūsara bhārgava* lineage in Dehra near Alwar. Rather than giving the date of his birth, it says that he became famous in 1734 CE (VS 1691). Then after a childhood spent in devotion, he moved to Delhi at the age of 12, when Shah Jahan was ruling there; by chance he met Śukdev and was initiated into the practice of *bhaktiyoga*. Due to his spirituality and pure wisdom, he was soon accompanied by a vast number of followers and during his lifetime came to have followers in every town. There then follows a story about how Shah Jahan decided to test him by sending him some baskets of sweets which were actually made of earth. However, Charaṇdās understood what was happening and miraculously turned them into real sweets and sent a gift of the very same sweets back to the Emperor, who was amazed to see the sweets when the basket was opened before him. Due to this and other matters he became famous. The author of the introduction also notes that one work in particular, the *Svārodaya*, a text for telling fortunes by observing the breath, had become very popular and was still popular. His followers included his sister Sahajo Bāī. He completed the *Bhaktisāgar* in CE 1724 (VS 1781) and passed away soon after that.

The reasons for the very different accounts of the life of Charaṇdās are unclear, but the two introductions indicate that views on the life of Charaṇdās were still far from fixed, even as late as the beginning of the twentieth century.

European Descriptions of Charaṇdās and his Followers

External references to Charaṇdās and his followers have appeared since the early nineteenth century in European accounts of Indian religious traditions, but a full picture was slow to emerge, despite the wealth of printed resources available. It is to these we must look for an account of the early development of the Charaṇdās movement itself.

The first reference was made in 1829 by H.H. Wilson, in an article that was to become part of his book *Hindu Religions, or An Account of the Various Religious Sects of India*. Wilson describes Charaṇdās as "a merchant of the Ḍhūsar tribe, who resided at Delhi in the reign of the second Alemgir." He describes the movement as "another Vaishnava sect," and its teachings as follows:

> Their doctrines of universal emanation are much the same as those of the Vedanta school, although they correspond with the Vaishnava sects in maintaining the great source of all things, or Brahma, to be Krishna: reverence of the Guru, and assertion of the preeminence of faith above every other distinction, are also common to them with other Vaishnava sects, from whom, probably, they differ in requiring no particular qualifications of caste, order, nor even of sex, for their teachers.

Wilson noted that originally the movement worshipped "no sensible representations of the deity," even the Tulasi plant or the salagram stone, although, he was informed, the followers had recently taken to such forms of worship "in order to maintain a friendly intercourse with the followers of Ramanand."

A strict morality was associated with a belief that actions "invariably meet with retribution or reward." The moral code included prohibitions against telling lies, slander, speaking harshly, discoursing idly, stealing, committing adultery, violence towards created things, imagining evil, cherishing hatred, or indulging in conceit and pride. Other obligations were the performance of one's professional and caste duties; association with pious persons; the placing of "implicit faith in the spiritual preceptor"; and the adoration of Hari as "the original and indefinable cause of all." Wilson also recorded that the followers of Charaṇdās were:

> both clerical and secular; the latter are chiefly of the mercantile order; the former lead a mendicant and ascetic life, and are distinguished by wearing yellow garments and a single streak of sandal, or Gopichandan, down the forehead; the necklace and rosary are of Tulasi beads; they also wear a small pointed cap, round the lower part of which they wrap a yellow turban. Their appearance in general is decent; and their deportment decorous.

In view of the "opulence" of the lay followers, Wilson felt that the monks were "well supported" in their ascetic existence.

Wilson further noted that "the authorities of the sect" are the *Shri Bhagavat* and *Gita*, there being "Bhasha translations" of both, and that parts of the former, at least, were ascribed to Charaṇdās himself. Wilson also reported that there were about twenty residents at the main centre in Delhi at that time, as well as five or six similar *maths* (monasteries) in Delhi, others in the upper Doab area, and that their numbers were rapidly increasing (Wilson 1904: 94-95).

In 1896, W. Crooke gave a more extensive account of Charaṇdās's life and of his followers (Crooke 1896: 201-204). His account was indebted to Wilson's work but also added the date of Charaṇdās's birth, 1703. He observed that Charaṇdās had, in fact, three successors, "Swami Ramrup, Gusain Jagatan and a woman named Shahgolai," each of whom had established a monastery and obtained recognition from first the Mughal, and then the British, governments. He then gave a summary of Wilson's account before adding his own notes, in which he commented that, unlike other dissenting sects, the Charaṇdāsis worshipped images, and that their literature was in the vernacular but showed considerable knowledge of Sanskrit. However, he reported that attempts by some learned followers to translate their literature into Sanskrit had been rejected by his other followers. The presence of works based on Sanskrit sources was also a notable feature of what he described as their "breviary," a short collection of sacred texts for daily use. In particular, one work was based on the puraṇas, and should have been called "Nasa Kshetra's Inferno." It contained a detailed description of what

'Nasa Kshetra' saw on a visit to hell and to heaven, and the relationship between particular sins and other actions on the destiny of the spirit after death. Crooke's account gave the number of Charaṇdās's mission teachers in the 1891 census as 161, mainly resident in the general area of Western Uttar Pradesh, with some 47 of them situated in Meerut.

In 1910 George Grierson gave a still more detailed account of Charaṇdās based on H.H. Wilson (1861), Powlett's Gazetteer of Ulwar (Simla 1880), MacLagan's Punjab Census Report for 1891 (Calcutta 1892), W. Crooke's *Tribes and Castes* (Calcutta 1896), and a work in Hindi by Devī Prasād in the *Nāgārī Pracāraṇī Sabhā Pattrikā* (Banaras, 1901). Grierson estimated that the number of Charaṇdāsī followers in the Punjab and UP numbered in some thousands. He included dates for both Charaṇdās's birth, 1703, and his death, 1782. Furthermore he reported that there were three main temples of his followers: at Bahādurpur in Alwar; at his birthplace, Ḍehra in Alwar; and in Delhi, the site of his death. With regard to his biography, Grierson suggests that Charaṇdās had said that he had lost his father at the early age of five; his father had gone into the forest to practise austerities and not returned. His mother then took him to Delhi where he met a holy man called Sukdeo Das from Muzaffarnagar who initiated him. Because Charaṇdās had a crippled foot, Śukdev gave him the name Charaṇ Dās ('servant of the feet'). Grierson describes how "the saint took the lame youth on his shoulders and after carrying him some distance, initiated him as a disciple, teaching him the Rama-mantra, or initiatory formula of the Rama-worshippers, and instructed him in faith in God (*Hari-bhakti*) and knowledge of the Supreme (*Brahma-jnana*)" (1910: 366). Charaṇdās then spent around twelve years in a cave practising austerities before founding his own sect around 1730.

Grierson mentioned the *Bhaktisāgar* of 1724 CE as being Charaṇdās's main work and noted the various editions published in Lucknow and Bombay in 1903. In addition, he noted that

Charaṇdās had made Hindi translations of the *Bhagavata Purāṇa; Bhagavadgīta; Jñānsvarodaya* (Delhi 1876); and *Nāsiketopākhyāna* (Bombay 1882), based on the story of Naciketas from the *Brahmāṇḍa Purāṇa*, itself based on the *Kaṭha Upanishad.* In addition to all of these, Grierson also noted that other editions of his verses had been published from Allahabad in 1908 (Grierson, 1910).

In 1911 H.A. Rose also mentioned the Charaṇdāsis briefly in a work on the Punjab and North Western Frontier Provinces; his information was, in part, based on MacLagan's Punjab Census Report for 1891. He included not only the factual information that was becoming standard by then but also information on the practices of Charaṇdās's followers, such as they kept the Ekadaśī lunar fasts, wore a particular sort of forehead mark and that they revered a text called the *Bhagat-sagar*. Rose also mentioned that there were stories of Charaṇdās having performed miracles before Nadir Shah when he conquered Delhi, and debated whether it was this that led to land grants being made to Charaṇdās and his followers (Rose, 1911: 37-38).

In 1920, F.E. Keay's history of Hindi literature covered most of the same facts as had previously been established. He also emphasized that Charaṇdās' teachings were basically like those of Kabīr, that he had been opposed to image worship, but that it had 'crept back into the sect' (Keay, 1920: 67). Keay commented that two of Charaṇdās's leading disciples had been women, Sahajo Bāī and Dayā Bāī. In 1984 Ronald Stewart McGregor summarized the previous studies and made further notes on Charaṇdās, Sahojo Bāī and Dayā Bāī in his history of Hindi literature (1984: 146-47).

The main contribution by Western scholarship on Charaṇdās was made by Daniel Gold, as part of his wider study of the *sants* in Northern India (1987). Gold's account included not only all the materials previously described in English sources but also materials gathered from field work in India and Hindi sources and also information derived from conversations with Śyamsundar

Śukla, see below, about the work he was doing which was published later in Hindi (Gold, 1987). In particular, Gold compares Charaṇdās' teachings with those of the eighteenth century sant Palṭū. He notes that both teachers had links to the trader community, Charaṇdās being a Ḍhūsar and Palṭū a *Kaṇḍū baniyā*, suggesting that *sant* traditions were becoming more accepted amongst twice born caste Hindus during the eighteenth and nineteenth centuries (Gold, 1992). Gold also draws attention to the yogic element in the verses of Palṭū and Charaṇdās, and comments on their complex allusions to the subtle centres, the yogic process of the reversal of the breath, and the union this practice creates between the self and the divine.

Recent Hindi Academic Studies

A scholarly interest in Charaṇdās by Hindi academic circles has developed from the nineteen thirties onwards. Part of the reason for this may have been that various features of his life posed questions about the relation of people from trader castes to the devotional *Sant* movement which challenged nationalist thinkers during this period.

Charaṇdās was included in Gaṇeśprasād Dvivedī's influential collection of works by *sant* authors, first published in 1939 by the Hindustani Academy in Allahabad, then later revised by Paraśuram Chaturvedī and regularly republished from 1952 to 1974. This work included a selection drawn from the Belvedere Press editions of verses published in 1908 and a brief introduction to his life, which described the broad outlines of the story, including his birth in Ḍehra in Alwar in a *Ḍhūsar* family in 1703. The story of how his father had disappeared in the forest while he practised austerities when Charaṇdās was only a child was also included. This story was then used as a way to contextualize Charaṇdās retiring to the forest himself to practise austerities and his meeting with the sage Śukdev who became his guru. Gaṇeśprasād also commented that Charaṇdās then moved to Delhi and lived there until his death in 1782.

Gaṇeśprasād reported that there were 52 main disciples but commented that principal amongst them were Sahajo Bāī and Dayā Bāī, who are still remembered as accomplished female spiritual practitioners. However, he said that Charaṇdās did not spread his teachings far and wide, and nor were his teachings very broad. Charaṇdās's teachings moreover, according to Gaṇeśprasād, were identical to those of Kabīr and focused on criticism of corruption in religious practices and traditions and on the emptiness of the teachings of the Vedas, Purāṇas and Smṛtī etc. Unfortunately, these analyses were made on the basis of the study of the only edition of Charaṇdās's works available to Gaṇeśprasād, the Belvedere Press edition. This edition is not typical of Charaṇdās's works and may have led to this biased impression; it contains teachings which stress the *sant* aspects in Charaṇdās's teachings, but does not include works which show his fondness for the worship of Radha and Kṛṣṇa, or his indebtedness to the Purāṇas and the Upaniṣads (Dvivedī, 1974: 254-70).

By the early 1950s much more had been learned about Charaṇdās within academic circles in India. The state of this knowledge was well depicted in Paraśurām Chaturvedī's influential and comprehensive history of the *sant* traditions (Chaturvedī, 1972: 718-28), first published in 1952. This book gave a detailed account of Charaṇdās' life, and also addressed the issues involved in various contradictory elements presented in some of the earlier accounts. For instance, the view put forward by Crooke that Charaṇdās's guru was a sage from Muzzafarnagar was countered by the claim in the works of Charaṇdās himself that his guru was the ancient sage Śukdeva. Chaturvedī also used the biographical materials composed by the followers of Charaṇdās, including the *Gurubhaktiprakāś* by Rāmrūp in 1769 CE and other works, to construct a much more detailed picture. He also reported on the tradition that by the end of Charaṇdās's life he had 52 prominent disciples, each of whom established their own centre of Charaṇdās' followers. His study of the works of Charaṇdās also much more accurately depicted the range of attitudes and teachings found in Charaṇdās's works than Gaṇeśprasād Dwīvedī had been able to do in 1939. Chaturvedī concluded his study with an account of the activities and areas in which Charaṇdās's followers were active, including: Delhi, UP, Eastern Punjab and Rajasthan.

Charaṇdās is undoubtedly one of the most outstanding of the Sants in the eighteenth century; he has left a remarkable legacy in both his works and his community of followers. However, some of the factors which led to his success in the eighteenth and nineteenth centuries, especially his drawing from both *nirguṇ* and *saguṇ* devotional traditions, and his appeal to merchant communities, have also led to problems in the twentieth century. Chaturvedī found it hard to reconcile Charaṇdās's role as a *sant* with the perceived behaviour of his followers in constructions of *sant* identity after independence in India. In particular, the principles of simplicity and non-possession which characterize Charaṇdās's teachings have remained largely unrealized in the lives of his followers. Beside this alleged lack of a special moral standing due to the limited perception of the purity of their conduct, Charaṇdāsis have seldom exhibited a desire for social reform, unlike, for example, the followers of Kabīr.

Allegories Based on Everyday Life in Sant Verses

That Charaṇdās's teachings appealed to a particular segment of Indian society is not unusual. There are many *sant* verses which use everyday activities as allegories for spiritual life based on topics such as farming, potting, spinning and weaving. These were used alike by non-trader community authors, such as Ravidās (1500-1550) and Kabīr, and trader community authors, like Palṭū and Dharamdās (1666-1708). One way to understand such verses is that they would have been appropriate when speaking to different audiences such as farmers, potters, spinners and weavers.

For instance, Kabīr used the following agricultural analogy to explain the nature of the spiritual life:

> The clouds are gathering in the sky, seekers, the clouds are gathering in the sky.
>
> Clouds are rising up in the east, rain is pouring down. Let each look after their own field boundary channels, let water flow in the channels.
>
> With mind as the bullocks, and mindfulness as the ploughman, plough the field of *nirvana*. Cast out the weeds of duality and sow the seed of the name (Kabir 1989a: 62)

There is also a famous traditional couplet attributed to Kabīr which draws upon the analogy of the potter and the clay to warn against pride:

> The clay said to the potter, 'Why do you press down hard on me?
> For the day is coming when I shall press down on you' (Traditional).

Spinning is another traditional everyday occupation which is used as an allegory by Kabīr:

> Mindfulness is the lover longing for the beloved spinning the spinning wheel.
>
> Spinning the beguiling beauty of the city of the body, with its palace for consciousness.
>
> Mindfulness is the girl who circles around the wedding fire in the heavens, around the seat of the jewel of wisdom.
>
> Thought is the spinning wheel strap. The three qualities are the spindle. The raw material is the mind's desires.
>
> The colours of the five and twenty-five are the cotton wool wads. The praising of the name is the skeins of cotton wool.
>
> Firm resolutions are the two pegs driven in. Yoga practices are the ridge pole.
>
> Fix the twelve names on the two petals, with the hammer of the essential word.
>
> Fine is the thread the seekers weave. Polished with the paste of loving devotion.
>
> Kabīr says, listen fellow seekers, from age to age this has been the true teaching. (Kabīr 1989b: 57)

A further important variety of these allegories which we will discus below are those concerned with the relationship of the spiritual life to the lives of members of the trader communities.

Traders in the Name of God

Gold has suggested that by the eighteenth century, the "preponderance of sants" were to be found among "members of the middle Hindu castes: those of traders and clean cultivators, most of the former identifying with the *vaiśyas*, 'merchants,' of classical times, and some of the latter with the *kṣatriyas*, 'warriors'" (1987: 62). He has also argued elsewhere that the use of imagery related to trade by Palṭū and Charaṇdās was representative of the ways in which *sant* traditions were becoming more accepted amongst twice born caste Hindus (Gold, 1992).

This juxtaposition of references to being a trader in the divine and yogic imagery is, however, much older than Palṭū and Charaṇdās; it had been a part of *sant* tradition since the time of Kabīr. There are also verses based on a similar trope of being a trader, *baipārī*, in the name of the divine, in the works of Kabīr's disciple, Dharmdās, who was also from a trader community:

> I am a trader in the true name.
> Some trade in copper and brass, some in cloves and betel.
> I trade in the wealth of the name, this in my sole cargo.
> Without breaking my capital my profit is fourfold,
> I have done great business.
> My market trading can't be halted,
> I trade in the street of freedom from fear.
> Drops of pearls well up in the body,
> the storehouse overflows with merit.
> Dharmdās the merchant, goes trading in the wealth of the name.
>
> (Dharmdās, 1985: 6)

There are also many verses addressed to a wandering trader, a *banjariyā*, about how life can be conceived of as lived in the four watches of the night. There are versions of this attributed to Ravidās (1500-1550), Dādūdāyal (1544-1603) and Guru Nānak (1469-1539). In Ravidās's version from the Fatehpur manuscript of 1582, the trader is conceived of as merchant who travels by sea:

> In the first watch of the night, what trade did you follow O *banjariyā*?
> You did not meditate on Hari Damodar, your childish mind was foolish.
> You fell into the trap of Maya and did not awaken.
> What use is there in repenting once you are at sea,
> If at first you did not set the sails?
>
> (Callewaert & Friedlander: 122-23)

There is a further verse by Ravidās, found in the Guru Granth (1603-4) and in Rajasthani manuscripts from before 1700, which begins:

> I am a trader (*banjariyā*) in Ram, I deal in *sahaj*.
> I have loaded the fortune of Ram's name, the world has loaded poison.
> The pass through the mountains is perilous,
> the only ox I have has no quality.
> Ram this is my one request, keep my capital safe, Murāri!
>
> (Callewaert & Friedlander, 1992: 149)

In a similar manner the analogy is drawn between the journey of the spirit and a trader on the sea of life in Dādūdāyal's verse:

> O Trader! In the third watch of the night you bore a heavy burden;
> your mind was led by *maya*, you never considered God at all.
> You never contemplated the divine, and did not take the name,
> so how could you be carried over the ocean of life?
> You could not cross over and began to repent as you sank into the flood. (Caturvedī, 1966: 504)

A verse attributed to Guru Nānak and found in a Rajasthani manuscript also uses this same allegory in order to stress how traders live their lives following *māyā* rather than *dharma*:

> O Trader! In the third watch of the night, your thoughts were on wealth and youth; O Soul! you did not consider Hari's name, and *māyā*'s company corrupted you. In passion for wealth and lust for youth, you wasted away your first life. You did not act in accor-

> dance with *dharma*, and did not think of Ram; Nānak says, in the third watch, your thoughts were on wealth and youth. (Śarmā, 1978: 36)

From these references it can be seen that imagery related to trading communities and activities have long been a part of a shared *sant* repertoire of imagery.

There were also numerous stories about traders, although not always complimentary, in the hagiographies of Kabīr, Ravidās and the other early *sants*. Taken as a whole, it can be suggested that the inclusion of allegories based on trading and stories about merchants in the hagiographies suggests that traders were always part of the audiences being addressed by *sant* teachers.

Early Circulation of Written Devotional Hindi Works

There have been various theories proposed for why trader and clean cultivator caste teachers and communities began to play an increasingly important role in *sant* traditions from the eighteenth century onwards. Jurgensmeyer (1995: 86) has suggested that trader communities, and in particular Khatrīs, were intent on improving their status in society and this made them sympathetic to the rhetoric of the *sants*.

A further factor may be that the trader communities were possibly prominent amongst the early patrons for written versions of the verses of the *sants*. Whilst the most studied manuscripts of verses attributed to the *sants* have been those copied at centres of various sant movements, such as those of the Dādūpanth, there were also a substantial number of copies of manuscripts of devotional works which do not have clear sectarian affiliations.

A study of Hindi manuscripts in the library of the Wellcome Institute in London has shown that in a number of cases devotional works were included among the works copied for merchants as composite manuscripts (often called *guṭkā* manuscripts). One clear instance of this practice is a manuscript of devotional works copied for a Jain merchant from Rajasthan, sometime between 1637 and 1698. Whilst this manuscript is not a collection of *sant* works, it does indicate that a reading public for religious works had started to develop in Rajasthan amongst merchant communities by the seventeenth century. Similar works in the eighteenth century also included manuscripts copied for patrons, who in some cases are women, in Jaisalmer, Jaipur, and Agra (Friedlander, 1996: 443-68).

The Impact of Charaṇdās's Personality

The factors mentioned above—tensions about caste status, the prevalence of existing tropes based on trader communities and the emergence of literate trader community audiences with a taste for written and later, printed, texts—may all have set the stage for the development of new traditions such as that of Dharmdās in the Kabīr Panth, and Charaṇdās.

Śyāmsundar Śukla has argued that the rapid spread of Charaṇdās's influence was due to his spiritual attainment gained through his practice of yoga, his high standards of conduct and thinking, and his inborn qualities. He was a persuasive and eloquent speaker, who excelled in combining disparate traditions into his teachings, thus proving attractive to followers from all castes and religions. These teachings were particularly broad. Charaṇdās's discourses incorporated elements of *sant nirguṇa* and yogic teachings, the worship of Radha and Kṛṣṇa, and also drew on Puranic and Upanishadic sources in Hindi vernacular forms. All of these factors led to his attracting thousands of followers during his lifetime (Śukla, 1995: 58-59). They continue to be attractive today as well. For instance, during the early 1970s, Osho Rajneesh gave a series of ten talks on Charaṇdās which was subsequently published as a book. In the first of these talks Osho commented that the greatness of Charaṇdās's teachings lay in part in the following message of spiritual equality: 'My guru told me, the devotees of Hari are his darlings, wherever one meets those beloved of Hari, then don't worry, don't make any distinction between Hindu, Muslim, Christian, Jain, Brahmin and Shudra' (Rajneesh 1978: 43).

In addition, however, despite his having lived recently enough to make it possible to construct a historical biography of his deeds, his attractiveness to his followers, in the past and still today, frequently relies on shared stories of supernatural events in his life, similar to those found in the hagiographies of other, earlier Indian spiritual teachers.

These stories include Charaṇdās 'initiating a lion' while he was still a child (Dās, 2000: 18-19); and the cycle of stories related to Nadir Shah, described above (Dās, 2000: 53-67). When Peter Friedlander visited the Charaṇdās' temple in Delhi in 2008, he was told the following story several times. Once, during the rainy season, a marriage party of members of the Khaṭīk community, who were followers of Charaṇdās, were attempting to return to Delhi. In order to do so, they needed to cross the Yamuna River near Agra, which was in flood. When the ferry finally set off, it contained around sixty members of the marriage party and around ten to fifteen of Charaṇdās's followers. Due to the storm, the boat began to sink in midstream. The boatmen told the marriage party that they would have to look after themselves. However, one of the devotees prayed to Charaṇdās to save them. Miraculously, the boat was lifted up and carried to the shore. It was said that Charaṇdās had manifested there without delay and carried the boat to the shore on his shoulder (Dās, 2000: 136-38).

The *Bhaktipadarth*

The *Bhaktipadarth* is the eighth of the twelve works included in the *Bhaktisāgar*. It is organized into twenty chapters of various lengths and complexity. Its key topics form a complex, logical and cohesive chain. The chapters deal in turn with the Guru; the devotees; sādhus; satsaṅg; God; devotion; the four great ages of the world; morality, immorality, and the mind; and, finally, after returning to the Guru and sādhus again, liberation.

This is the logic of lived experience, not of any abstract philosophy deducing the seen universe from an unseen and unknowable God. In this logic, the Guru and the spiritual community of fellow worshippers come first. The rest follows from this. Charaṇdās presents the teachings of *The Treasury of Devotion* as not his own but deriving from those of his own Master, Śukdev. Everything he has to say owes its authority to Śukdev.

The teacher matters because he (or she) allows the disciple "to serve/ The lotus feet of the Lord," thus opening the way to liberation, the ending of countless births, deaths and rebirths, together with all the suffering this involves.

The personal characteristics of the True Guru are described in Part III of Chapter 1. He is:

A sage who is
Independent,
Undeluded,
Uncorrupted,
Continually wandering,
Careful,
Enlightened,
Free from doubt.

A sage who knows the truth,
Who is satisfied,
Wise,
Keeps the company of the saints.
He never begs.
He is never proud.
He is dispassionate,
Stable,
Gentle of speech.

Tranquil and humble,
Free of karma,
Without attachments,
Whose mind is at rest;
Such a man, O Lord,
Is my own true Guru. (43-44)

The guru does not always seem to be "gentle of speech." Part 5 of the same chapter describes the True Guru in violent military terms: his word is variously compared to "cannon balls," "arrows," "swords," "spears," and "barbed arrows." These images may have appealed to those followers who identified with warrior values. What the guru destroys, in fact, is the disciple's ego:

The disciple's death
Lasts a lifetime.
Struck by the Guru,
He goes beyond.
The sense of self
Vanishes. (47)

The guru has a double relationship with the divine. Firstly, he stands between the disciple and God, protecting the disciple from divine wrath:

Do not be afraid—
If Hari is angry,
The Guru will save you.
Always think of the Guru,
Be attentive to him. (54)

On the other hand, the guru does not just point to the divine but actually IS "Rām . . . Kṛṣṇa . . . Narasiṅgha . . . Vāmana . . . The manifest form of God." Or, paradoxically, the Guru is even greater than God:

Hari is greater
Than any mother.
The Guru is greater
Than Hari. (52)

How can this be? Charaṇdās does not really explain, but his disciple Sahajo Bāī does, in the remarkable eleventh poem of the *Sahaj Prakāś*:

I might leave Rama, I could never forget my Guru.
In my eyes, Hari is not the equal of my Master.
Hari brought me into this world,

The Guru freed me from the cycle of birth and death.

Hari sent five thieves with me,
The Guru released me from their power.
Hari entangled me in the web of my family,
The Guru broke the chains of attachment.

Hari bound me with disease and the love of life,
The Guru made me a yogi and freed me from this.
Hari confused me with karma and dharma,
The Guru showed me my own soul.

Hari hid himself from me,
The Guru gave me a lamp and showed me God.
Above all, Hari created the bondage of sweet maya,
But the Guru removed me from all these illusions.

I offer my body and mind to Charaṇdās,
I will never leave my Guru, I might leave Hari.

(Trans. Aveling and Joshi, 2001: 13)

The disciple's duty and privilege is to serve the Guru. Serving the Guru is quick. Charaṇdās declares:

I served Hari
For sixteen years.
I served the Guru
Only four seconds.
The Vedas declare:
There was no comparison. (40)

It is also efficacious; in fact, far more efficacious than other methods:

Yoga, almsgiving,
Bathing at sacred sites,
Are all fruitless, unless
You serve the Guru. (42)

In *The Treasury of Devotion* the members of the community, "clerical and secular" are respectively described as "sādhus" and "devotees," although the terms often seem interchangeable:

Those who have seen the Sādhus

Do not care about death.
Those who bow to the devotees
Will not suffer when they die. (57)

The two groups are marked by their being bound to the Master and to each other. Their characteristics, as described in Chapter 3, are similar to those of the Guru:

Purified, loving, worshipful,
Satisfied, perpetually wandering,
Mind fixed in the nine forms of devotion,
Knowing no other desires.

Merciful, generous, virtuous,
Honorable, resolute in speech.

I have no desire for liberation,
For realization, perfection or renunciation. (59)

The Guru and all classes of devotees meet together in *satsang*, the devotional gathering of the holy ones to sing hymns and chant the Name together. Chapter 5 provides two completely different perspectives on such gatherings. The first is from below: the poem presents a garland of low caste persons who have been saved through *satsang*—including Vālmiki, Sābarī, Dhanna, Kabīr, Raidās, Kuva, "Saina the barber," Kubari and Suva who "was liberated by a prostitute." The other perspective is from above: "The gods are saved/ By the company of Sādhus."

Alone, the devotees are absorbed in meditation, chanting the Name far into the night, while using the breath to raise the consciousness from the belly to the crown of the head. A final summary of these teachings on meditation occurs at the very end of the *Treasury of Devotion*:

I am a citizen
Of the realm of emptiness.
My family deity is the unstruck sound.
My lineage is the unchanted chant.
Charaṇdās says: "This is my secret." (219)

The *Bhaktipadarth* has little room for stories of major Hindu deities, or even of Rādha and Kṛṣṇa who feature so strongly in the earlier books of the the *Bhaktisāgar*. Charaṇdās's image of God, especially in Chapter 6, places particular emphasis on the mystery of Divine power and on the utter unknowability of God. The description begins on a fairly concrete level: God can do anything, even the most contradictory things:

He can save a blade of grass,
In a burning forest fire.
He can fit the ocean
Into a tiny pitcher. (68)

After describing many more manifestations of the paradoxical divine will, Charaṇdās slowly begins to move towards a contemplation of God in negative terms:

How can I praise Him
Whatever I say He is,
He is not. (73)

He has "no beginning,/ Middle or end./ No front, back, left or right," age, gender, name, form or action. God is both beyond everything and yet somehow still in everything as well:

'He is manifest,'
'He is unmanifest . . .'
He is neither of these.
However you conceive Him to be,
He is not that either,
No matter how many times you try. (76)

And yet, the divine also plays "infinite, indivisible./ Endless games," in which He takes "infinite/ Beautiful forms" as the twenty-four incarnations of Vishnu "To overcome evil,/ And uphold the saints" (compare *Bhagavad Gita*, 8: 4). Here too there is a paradox:

Oh Charaṇdās, His form
Is incomparable.
Ram is like Ram.

That is all I can say. (73)

The text thus affirms both *nirguṇa* and *saguṇa* experiences while placing both in the realm of paradox and unknowability.

Charaṇdās emphasized three aspects of the spiritual life in his teachings: knowledge, yoga and devotion (following the *Shrimad Bhagavatam*). Devotion is the most important of these and has "nine aspects—hearing, chanting, remembering, serving, worship, prostration, obedience, friendship and self-dedication." It is the most suitable path for the Kali Yuga [chapter 10].

The second half of the book is given over to the consideration of the role of morality in developing or destroying devotion—practical teachings for clerics and lay people alike. A brief formula to which Charaṇdās refers a number of times is "gold and girls," which we have generally translated more broadly as "material and sensual desires." Following traditional lists of the major vices, Charaṇdās is also content to note that there are "five hungry ghosts" which "will ruin yoga, austerity and devotion." They are lust, anger, delusion (or infatuation), greed and pride. Charaṇdās gives long and strict discussions of each of these vices in Chapter 12, then provides ways of overcoming them in Chapter 13: namely, the practices of morality (translated here as "virtue") and compassion. Chapter 15 returns to vice and virtue, this time through a consideration of the Mind, and the senses of sight, hearing, taste, touch, and smell (which are, of course, aspects of the mind in Hindu thought). The task of the mind is to free itself from sensual objects, through continual meditation on Hari and "the lotus feet of the Master." Charaṇdās concludes:

I have sung this *Treasury of Devotion*
And revealed certain secrets.
Whoever understands these things with love
Will be freed from death's snare.
If you contemplate it regularly,
Says Guru Śukdev,

You will pass over
The ocean of existence. (219-20)

Devotion to the *Bhaktisāgar* (The Ocean of Devotion)

An indication of the role that the *Bhaktisāgar* plays in the life of the followers of Charaṇdās can be seen in a work by Saras Mādhurī on how it should be honoured and the manner for its recitation, which is found as one of the introductory works in an edition of *Bhaktisāgar* published from Jaipur.

This short work was composed by a prominent Charaṇdāsī Sant called Saras Mādhurī who lived from CE 1855-1926 (VS 1912-1983). He was a prolific author with many followers in the Charaṇdāsī Sampradāya, who was influential in Vrindavan, Jaipur, Rivari and Dehra and greatly respected by figures such as Naresh Sawai Madhav Singh, king of Jaipur, and the king of Kishangarh. He was a pioneer in publishing print editions of works related to the Charaṇdāsī tradition (Śukla 313-15). One of the works he published was a print edition of the *Bhaktisāgar* which was reprinted from time to time at the Jaipur Centre of the Charaṇdāsī Sampradāya up to an edition which was published in CE 1999 on the 101st anniversary of the birth of his disciple and successor Rasik Mādhurī.

From this text it can be seen that the *Bhaktisāgar* played in some senses a similar role amongst the followers of Charaṇdās to that played by the *Bījak* for followers of Kabīr and the *Guru Granth Sāhib* amongst the Sikhs. It was, and is, honoured as if it was the living presence of the guru and treated with similar devotion in the practice of readings from it as part of regular devotional practice. As an introductory part of daily practice the following text can be read: "The manner for the recitation of the text *The Ocean of Devotion*:

Sants listen with attention to my entreaty,
    I bow to you and fold my hands in salutation.
That I may explain to you how to read the text,
    as I have heard so I sing again.
Make yourself pure, sacred and free from worry,

sit alone with mind resolved.
Place the king of texts upon a stand,
offer up to it sandalwood and flowers.
Set your heart on Śri Śuk Charaṇdās,
and devote yourself to his feet.
First read the work in praise of the greatness of the text,
then read the text itself.
Read it out in a natural sweet voice,
drenched in the hue of loving devotion.
With a one pointed mind contemplate its meaning,
read and recite it and hold it in your heart.
Oh brother, after reading it,
sing the *ārati* verse with joy.
Read it everyday and serve Hari the guru,
don't eat or drink until you have read it.
Look after the text as dearly as your life,
regard it as your object of devotion and sing its praises.
This is a fortune from the mouth of the guru,
don't abandon the text even at the cost of your life.
As a duty recite it every day,
don't fix your mind on anything else.
Read it every day according to the rites,
you will attain the four aims, liberation and the eight perfections.
If you follow this manner of living,
you will be called a true sant and great soul.
Perform the songs in praise of the divine couple,
you will definitely attain the divine abode.
Saras Mādhurī has sung this,
just as explained to him by his Guru Baldevdās.

"The manner for the recitation of the text 'The Ocean of Devotion' composed by Saras Mādhurī the disciple of Svāmī Baldevdās" (Charaṇdās 1999: 4).

Our Translation

Our text of the *Bhaktipadarth* is based on a critical reading of three printed versions of the text: the Avadhasamacār Press edition (ca. 1903), the Śrīveṅkateśvār edition (2001) and an edition published by Saras Mādhuri Śaraṇ (1999) from the Jaipur centre of the *Charaṇdāsī panth.* A detailed study of the various editions of the works of Charaṇdās was published in 1992 by Kranti Kumar Caturvedi (Caturvedi 1992), but we have not been able to locate this particular work. However, we found that the last edition of the *Bhaktipadarth* we consulted contained a number of sections found in neither the Avadhasamacār Press edition nor the Śrīveṅkateśvār edition, and therefore we have not translated these sections. In general the first two editions consulted contained very similar readings which we have adopted as the Hindi text which forms the basis for our translation.

The Treasury of Devotion is written in verse. It generally uses two and four line verse forms (*dohā* and *chaupai*), but also includes a few other forms as well (*aṣtapadi, kavitta, arilla* and *kuṇḍali* metres). These verses mainly consist of religious and moral teachings, but also include several longer narratives as well as many brief references to stories of the lives of exemplary devotees with which its listeners would have been familiar. Overall, our aim has been to produce a simple and pleasant free verse translation, built around the stresses placed on key words in Charaṇdās's conventional lines.

The only English translation of another complete work by Charaṇdās so far published has been that of the *Aṣṭāṅgayogavarṇan* by Om Prakash Tiwari (1983). However, there have also been two volumes of translations of works by Charaṇdās's disciples: the *Sahaj Prakāś,* translated by Harry Aveling and Sudha Joshi (2001), and the *Songs of Daya Bai,* translated by Harry Aveling and Peter Friedlander (2005).

Conclusion

The story of perceptions of Charaṇdās since the eighteenth century reveals the ways in which religious identities are constantly negotiated and still remain in flux within devotional traditions in India. It is to be hoped that further translations of Charaṇdās's works into English, such as is being attempted here, will stimulate greater interest in understanding Charaṇdās's role in the development of religious traditions in North India from the eighteenth century to the present day.

Peter Friedlander and Harry Aveling
Melbourne
December 2013

Sant Charaṇdās: *Treasury of Devotion*

Chapter 1: The Greatness of the Guru

I pray to you,
Vyasa, honored sage,
Come dwell in my heart.
Only you can help me
Explain devotion's treasure.

Give me the wisdom
Steeped in love
That grants success in yoga.
Charaṇdās prays:
Hear me, again and again.

You give everything,
I am a beggar.
Merciful Śukdev,
Give me devotion,
Dispel my distress,
Remove my worries.

I was useless,
My body was worthless;
Through the grace of Guru Śukdev,
My body became precious.

Who was I?
No one knew.
Through the grace of Guru Śukdev,

I learned to serve
The lotus feet of the Lord.

No one looked at me.
No one touched my shadow.
Through the grace of Guru Śukdev,
I drank the nectar
Of the Lord's lotus feet.

I was the son of a Ḍhūsar—
Devoid of devotion,
A beggar.
Through the grace of Guru Śukdev
Hari made me rich,
Took away my cares.

There is a treasure
Tricksters can't touch,
Which cannot be hoarded,
Thieves cannot steal,
Which cannot be lost.

I dedicated myself to my Guru,
My mind continually returned to Him.
In an instant
I merged with Brahma.
I was a fool,
Then I was found.

I served Hari
For sixteen years.
I served the Guru
Only four seconds.
The Vedas declare:
There was no comparison.

A Sādhu knows
How to serve the Guru,
A fool does not.
How could a fool
Serve the Guru?
Serving the Guru
Is beyond everything else.
Know this,
Men and women.

Serving the Guru
Destroys obstacles,
Dispels distress,
Removes sin.
Serving the Guru
Ends the 84 lakh lives,
Breaks the chains of rebirth.

Serving the Guru
Frees us from death,
Kills selfish love,
Awakens devotion.
Serving the Guru
Illuminates love
Intoxicates the heart
Destroys worldly desires.

Serving the Guru,
I saw Paramatma;
Beyond the three gunas
I saw the Fourth.
Śukdev told me the secret.
Charaṇdās, serve the Guru.

II

Not knowing
How to serve the Guru,
I didn't worship him
Or adore his feet.
Yoga, almsgiving,
Chanting and austerities,
Nothing worked at all.

Yoga, almsgiving,
Bathing at sacred sites,
Are all fruitless, unless
You serve the Guru.
If you do not serve the Guru,
You will suffer
Again and again
When you reach death's door.

Without serving the Guru,
You will suffer:
Be born in poverty,
An animal.
Without serving the Guru,
No one can be liberated,
Saved from the ocean of existence.

Without serving the Guru,
Fool, what will you do?
Whose boat will you ride
To the other shore?
Nothing succeeds;
Without serving the Guru,
You will fall
Into a deep dark well.

Without serving the Guru,
The body lies in darkness.
How can the light of wisdom
Ever shine?
Charaṇdās served Guru Śukdev,
He who destroys hell.

A man who conquers the senses,
Who hates no one,
Has no illusions,
Knows no conflict.
In the shelter of such a Guru,
All suffering and distress are destroyed.

III

A Guru who favours no one,
Hates no one,
Can save his disciple;
He destroys hopes, desires and malice;
Makes pleasant
Body, mind and speech.

A sage who is
Independent,
Undeluded,
Uncorrupted,
Continually wandering,
Careful,
Enlightened,
Free from doubt.

A sage who knows the truth,
Who is satisfied,

Wise,
Keeps the company of the saints.
He never begs.
He is never proud.
He is dispassionate,
Stable,
Gentle of speech.

Tranquil and humble,
Free of karma,
Without attachments,
Whose mind is at rest;
Such a man, O Lord,
Is my own True Guru.

IV

Honest and courteous,
Stout hearted, a True Yogi,
Firm in meditation
Established in the Supreme Consciousness—
Put your faith
In such a Guru.

Destroying delusions,
Removing fears
Dispelling doubts,
Dispensing wisdom
With open hands—
Make such a man
Your Guru.

I will tell you
The qualities of the True Guru,
So you can recognize him.

Use your body, mind, wealth,
Your life,
To find and test such a man.

While you live,
Before you die,
Give him your desires,
From one life to the next,
So he can purify you.

Go to his side.
Accept his blows.
Sparks will fly from his anvil
And burn all your chaff.

The True Guru
Is a mighty warrior.
He strikes with his words;
His cannon balls are love,
He storms the castle of illusion.

His words announce the attack.
Sentries may tire of the wind,
The ears never tire of his words.
The True Guru
is a skilled archer.
I am the deer,
The Teacher is the hunter.
His word is the arrow.
Charaṇdās fell wounded,
Pierced in body, mind, life.

The sword of his word
Struck me,
Tore through my heart.

Śukdev struck the swan.
He would never abandon me.

His word is a sword
Which tears the body apart.
Cowards turn and run,
Warriors face him
And take his blows.

The True Guru's word
Is a spear.
The Sādhu can withstand it.
Cowards run away;
They are destroyed.

The True Guru's word
Is an arrow,
It pierces
Body and mind.
If you have no heart
It won't hurt you.
Lovers in separation
Know the secret.

The True Guru's word
Is a barbed arrow.
It enters the body
And can never leave.
The pain of love
Is sweet.

The True Guru's word
Is his arrow.
It will cut off your legs.
You will fall

On the battlefield of love
And never rise again.

The True Guru's word
Cleaves you completely.
The lover struggles
On the field of battle
And holds nothing back.

The disciple's death
Lasts a lifetime.
Struck by the Guru,
He goes beyond.
The sense of self
Vanishes.
His form
Is the divine essence.

Killed by the True Guru,
His life is over.
He is never reborn.
He is Hari's,
Forever.

Killed by the words
Of the True Guru,
He is fortunate.
The disciple rises
Beyond the three qualities,
Beyond attraction and aversion.

Struck by the sword
Of the True Guru,
The disciple no longer cares
About kings' fortunes,

Diamonds, pearls,
Wives, sons,
Horses, elephants
Hunting falcons.

Struck by the wise words
Of the True Guru,
Food has no flavour,
Rebirth in Indra's heaven
Promises only pain,
Oh Charaṇdās!

I searched and found
The True Guru.
Nothing else
Satisfied me.
When the disciple
Is dedicated to the Guru
Everything else
Is dust.

Rank, caste,
Family, life-stage,
Pride, achievements,
Disappear.
When you find the feet
Of the True Guru,
You become
His own disciple.

Bow your head
Before the Guru.
Say: Master,
Take away
My sins and sorrow.

I am your servant,
I depend on you.
Let me dwell at your feet.
I offer you
My mind and body.
I desire
Nothing else.

Whatever you want,
Do that.
Fill me
However you wish.
Put me in the sun
Or in the shade,
Drive me mad
Or liberate me.

Manly virtues, intellect,
I have none.
I take refuge in you
In every way.
I was lost,
You found me.
Wherever I go,
I will go with you.

I sit in your boat.
Take me across
The river of my desires.
Pull me out
From the whirlpool of delusion.
I join my hands
And bow before you.

Go to the Guru,
Say these words.
Hold nothing back,
Speak sincerely.
Open your heart
And tell him:

I give you my self;
Put me
Wherever you want.
Charaṇdās stands at your door.
Scold me as much as you want.

I do not need
Riches, perfection and great deeds;
They belong to the world.
I come to you
With empty hands.

My only desire
Is to repeat your name.
I do not want to be a king
Or to live in Indra's heaven.

Rebirth brings great suffering,
I seek refuge in you.
I desire liberation.
I fear rebirth.

I bow at your feet
In devotion to Ram,
Only one thing I ask:
Flood my heart
With love and joy.

Make me your own,
Lead me always.
Place your hand on my head,
You are my Master.
Take Charaṇdās,
Save him.
I am an egg,
Brood over me.

If the egg falls before its time,
The Guru will pick it up.
Make me your own,
Again and again.
Free your disciple from doubt.

V

Make me your own
Let me serve you in three ways:
In devotion,
As the monkey clings to its mother.
In knowledge,
As the tree grows in the forest.
In meditation,
As the turtle withdraws into its shell.

If a baby is separated from its mother
—Even for a second—
It will soon become dirty.
Charaṇdās says:
Be attentive to the Guru.

The mother looks after the child
Much better than the father can.
She may scold and cajole

But never stops loving her baby.

If the child speaks roughly,
She will bless him with a laugh.
The Guru serves
All those who bow before him.

Hari is greater
Than any mother.
The Guru is greater
Than Hari.
Śukdev told me:
His love
Will remove all your faults.

I am like clay
In the hands of the potter.
He works the outside
In order to perfect the inside.

As soon as Śukdev saw me,
I was freed.
Everything changed
The crow became a swan.

The Guru was merciful,
Broke my pride and ego,
Wiped away gluttony and lust
Gave me peace.

The True Guru was kind:
He opened my eyes
And showed me
That world was false.
The body

Can never be at peace.

VI

I tell you:
Believe only
In the Guru.
Charaṇdās
Contemplates
This truth.

The Guru
Is the Vedas;
He manifests
The myths.
The Guru
Is the Teacher;
He manifests
Their meaning.

The Guru is Shiva
And Shesanaga,
Fix your awareness on him.
The Guru is Brahma
And Vishnu,
He fills the empty.

The Guru is the Wishing-tree
That satisfies all of our desires.
The Guru is the Wishing-cow
Who grants all our needs.

Like the Ganges,
The Guru washes away our sins.
Like Shiva,

The Guru cools our fevered longings.

Like the sun,
The Guru drives away darkness.
The Guru is the Supreme God,
Who makes us free.

Contemplate the Guru,
Chant his name.
Give yourself to him,
Worship your Guru.
The all-knowing Śukdev said:
Praise him
Even though you cannot.
Bow at his feet.

Do not be afraid—
If Hari is angry,
The Guru will save you.
Always think of the Guru,
Be attentive to him.

Do not abandon the Guru
To serve Hari.
Those who run away
Cannot hide,
Even in hell.

He who criticizes the Guru
Will never be liberated.
He will be reborn
84 lakh times
And always find suffering.

Study the Guru,

Examine him carefully,
Then fall at his feet.
Contemplate him.
Place your trust in him.

Know him as Ram,
The equal of Kṛṣṇa,
An incarnation of Narasingha,
Know him as Vamana.

Know him as the fulfiller,
The manifest form of God.
Know him as everything,
The one beyond compare.

Know beyond doubt
That the Guru and Hari are one.
He drives away
The burden of bad thoughts.

He is your father in the dharma,
He will make you strong.

Hold this teaching in your heart.
Hold his feet in your mind.
Serve him resolutely.
Even if he scolds you a thousand times,
Do not turn away from him.
Love the Guru. Abandon all others.

The true disciple gives himself completely.
Understand and accept Charaṇdās's teachings.

Śukdev explained this to me.
It is taught in the Vedas and Puranas.

Charaṇdās asks himself:
How can I fully praise the Guru?

Now I will speak of the devotees,
The purifying company of the holy ones.

Chapter 2: The Greatness of the Devotees

I praise the devotees,
Who please my body, mind and heart.
Their consciousness shines brightly,
Despite the dark filth of the Kali Yuga.

Charaṇdās serves the Sādhus
He fixes his mind on them.
They have broken the bonds of birth and death.
They are untouched by worldly ills.

Whoever serves the devotees
Will escape death's snare.

Those who have seen the Sādhus
Do not care about death.
Those who bow to the devotees
Will not suffer when they die.

Those who enjoy the company of Sādhus
Will not burn in the fires of hell.
Those who praise the Sādhus
Will taste loving devotion.

Those who love the devotees
Will make Hari their own.

Those who sing the songs of the devotees
Will gain the supreme state.

There is no liberation

Unless one keeps company with the holy ones.

Why be an ascetic? Why live in silence?
Charaṇdās says: I will take the shelter of the devotees,
Whether I live, whether I die.

Chapter 3: The Characteristics of the Devotee

Purified, loving, worshipful,
Satisfied, perpetually wandering,
Mind fixed in the nine forms of devotion,
Knowing no other desires.

Merciful, generous, virtuous,
Honorable, resolute in speech.

I have no desire for liberation,
For realization, perfection or renunciation.

Profit and loss mean nothing to him;
Friendship or enmity, the false or the real.

He knows nothing of fame or blame,
Is indifferent to suffering and pleasure.

Why care about good luck or bad?
A king and the beggar are the same.

Gold is no better than brass.
Worldly ways mean nothing.

No victory or defeat, no arguments.
Forever holy, beyond our understanding.

He experiences neither joy nor sorrow.
He loves all forms of life.

Śukdev told Charaṇdās:

These are the marks of the Sādhu.

II

The status of the devotee
Is higher than Indra.
Renouncing the three worlds,
He takes Hari as his own.

He is always devoted, never attached.
He does not long for fourfold liberation
Or even for Vaikuntha. Oh Charaṇdās,
He is free from all attachments.

Chapter 4: The Greatness of the Sādhus

The Lord himself said:
The Sādhus are My body.
I love the dust of their feet.

They don't care for spiritual powers,
For gold or for girls.
They prefer My company
And will never leave Me.

They have renounced everything
To love and praise Me.
I am given into their hands
And am glad that this is so.

Sādhus are my soul.
They love Me.
Narada, you decide,
Is this true or not?

I made this amazing world
For their sake.
I am born into this world in every age
To satisfy their desires.

I am indebted to them.
Fourfold liberation
Is the interest I pay,
Beyond all price.

Out of love,

I give everything
To my devotees.
I have even manifested Myself
In the body of animals.

My people live in Me
And I live in them.
There is no difference
Between Myself and My saints.

I sleep
Where My Sādhus sleep.
I eat
Where my Sādhus eat.
When they sing,
I clap with them.

They sing
Wherever they go;
I sing with them.
I protect them
Wherever they go.
Their love
Fills My bowl.

My hand is over them
Wherever they walk.
I will never abandon them
Wherever they wander.

Those who serve the devotees
Rule over Me.
I live in them,
So great is My love.

Wherever they walk
Is more blessed than any pilgrimage site.
Hari told Charaṇdās this:
Their feet hallow the earth.

The Lord Himself
Sings their greatness.
Who can equal them?
The Vedas glorify them.

The gods in heaven
Long to be Sādhus.
They serve the devotees
So they can see them.

They rejoice
In each and every world.
Where do they go
When they leave their bodies?

Fortunate the city, the land,
The town, hamlet or village,
Where they are born.
I honor those places.

The devotees are born into this world
For the sake of the truth.
They save themselves and others.
They adorn the realm of devotion.

They liberate countless beings
From the ocean of existence.
Sādhus are Ram's ferrymen;
They take us to the Beloved.

Sādhus renounce pride,
Lust, anger, passion and greed.
They worship Ram
With all their being.

Who can praise the Sādhus?
Their splendor is incomparable.
Even Sesha's two thousand tongues
Would not be enough to honor them.

The greatness of their loving devotion
Wins Govinda's heart.
Charaṇdās says:
Pure bliss is mine.

Chapter 5: In Praise of Satsang

I waited a thousand years
For a moment of satsang.
Śukdev knew
I could wait no longer.

Smriti, the Vedas and the Puranas
Sing of the greatness of satsang.
Sage Vasistha revealed this secret:
The gods are saved
By the company of Sādhus.

In the company of Sādhus,
Narada recalled his past lives.
Valmiki and Sabari saw the greatness of satsang
And sang of its glory.

Ajamila was saved by satsang,
It burned away all his faults.
Countless sinners have found liberation,
Saved by satsang.

Dhanna, Kabir and Raidas
Were enlightened through satsang.
Śukdeva told Charaṇdās:
They were saved by satsang.

Whenever you want a vision of Ram
Ask for satsang.
Seek to be dyed
In the ninefold colors of devotion.

Kuva, Saina and Sadna the barber
Were low caste folk
Raised up high.
Puddles and brooks become holy
When they merge
With the Ganges.

A wooden boat
Can carry objects of iron.
The company of holy ones
Can carry sinful mortals
Across the ocean of existence.
Touched by the philosopher's stone,
Iron becomes gold.
It is truly blessed.

You can travel to temples,
Go on pilgrimages,
Without the company of Sādhus
You will never be saved.

The leaves of the *dhak* tree,
The seeds of the *pan*,
Are dignified
In the company of kings.

Kubari sang with Govinda,
Suva was liberated by a prostitute.
Oh Hari! Charaṇdās begs:
Let me live with the Lord,
Life after life.

Gods, men, sages,
Are humbled at the sight

Of the Sādhu.
The Sādhu's greatness
Is beyond words.

II

Sarang Raga

Narahari, be with your devotees,
Increase our joy, remove our sorrows,
Help us drop our desires. Be with the saints,
Who seek the wealth of the Name.
Whoever finds the Name is freed
From sin, and is overwhelmed with wisdom.
If you are merciful to the saints,
They will offer you love's *bhang*.
Their clear vision makes Hari's eyes shine.
Take refuge at their feet, serve them
And be glad. Oh Charaṇdās!
The Ganges longs to touch their feet.

Chapter 6: The Greatness of God

Beyond existence,
Hari does it all.
Within existence,
He is spirit.
Charaṇdās offers himself
In worship
And goes beyond his body.

To see Hari
Is to see the truth.
Leaving your family
Matters not.

Whatever he wants,
He does.
No matter how difficult,
It is within His power.

He can save a blade of grass,
In a burning forest fire.
He can fit the ocean
Into a tiny pitcher.

He can keep a flame alive
Under the waters.
He can build an ocean
Where there is no world.

He can float a mountain
On the sea.

He can make wood
Sink into the depths.

He can lead an elephant
Through the eye of a needle.
He can grow a tree
Without roots and leaves.

He can suckle a baby
At a man's breast.
He can grow crops
On a field in the sky.

If He wanted,
A dumb man could recite the Vedas,
A blind man
Could see the light.

Śukdev told Charaṇdās:
He is all powerful,
He can fulfill
All our desires.

Whatever the Lord wants,
He does.
Who can stop Him?
Behold!
Wonder after wonder,
Charaṇdās was amazed.

II

Murari built a palace
On the wind.
He made a waterfall

In a raging fire.

If He wishes,
Rain will fall
From a clear sky.
The sun will be darkened
But the day
Will be bright.

The empty will be full,
The full empty.
Whatever He desires
Can happen.

Stones can float.
Oceans can vanish
In an instant.

He can calm the sea
And turn a mountain
Into a mustard seed.

He can make a beggar into a king
And sweep away monarchs.

Whatever He wants
He can do.
The wishes of others
Mean nothing to Him.

Charaṇdās sings
Of the true nature of God.
Śukdev taught me this.

I praise the Creator,

Who made the universe.
Constantly manifesting
Countless miracles,
In an unfathomable, unsurpassable,
Cosmic drama.

III

Creating, sustaining, destroying,
Revealing infinite suns and moons.

Creating thousands of universes in an instant.
If He wanted, everything could vanish.

Expanding into infinite forms.
Contracting into the one.

Playing with the seeds of the banyan tree;
The whole creation from a single seed.

In that one seed are countless seeds.
Countless shapes and forms.

Such is Hari, manifest as the world.
I stand in awe, speaking,
Hearing and seeing,
Only Him.

Contemplating Him,
Over and over again.
Trying to understand Him.
Charaṇdās bows before God.

The ocean of His deeds
Cannot be fathomed.

I do not have the words.
Charaṇdās says:
When I think of His deeds,
I am lost in wonder.

IV

Thousands of Brahmas
Sing His praise.
The Vedas say:
The Lord is the highest of all.

Thousands of Shivas
Meditate on Him.
They cannot understand
His endless form.

Thousands of Naradas
Sing His praise.
They cannot grasp
His endless virtues.

Thousands of meditators
Think of Him.
They cannot understand
Hari's form.

Thousands of scholars
Debate wisdom.
Exhausted
They still don't understand Him.

Thousands of Saradas
Contemplate Him.
Their intellect tires.

He is incomparable.

Gods, men, sages,
No one understands His secret.
They search and search
To no avail.

Manifest, unmanifest,
He cannot be described.
Charaṇdās says,
Śukdev told me this:

Oh Charaṇdās, His form
Is incomparable.
Ram is like Ram.
That is all I can say.

V

How can I praise Him?
Whatever I say He is,
He is not.

I'm puzzled, perplexed.
Defeated. Exhausted.
And still know nothing.

He has no beginning,
Middle or end.
No front, back, left or right.

He is not green or yellow,
White or black.
Neither man nor woman, young or old.

Beyond all names,
Forms and actions,
Neither light nor heavy.

Beyond the four texts
That tell of nirvana.
Beyond all knowing.

More subtle
Than the fragrance of a flower.
Guru Śukdev taught me this.

Who can see?
Who can say?
Astonishing. Invisible. Unknowable.
Beyond wisdom,
Beyond meditation,
Free of change and imperfection.

This is the wonder I saw.
He has no voice
No form and no body.

Neither with form
Or without form.
Neither moving nor static.

Beyond the five elements
And three qualities.
Extraordinary wonder,
No mind can contemplate.

Neither manifest
Nor hidden.
I can't understand

And it exhausts me to try.

Whenever I say:
He is like this,
I immediately realize
He is not like that at all.

When I say:
He is not like this,
Then I see Him
In everything.

Śukdev told Charaṇdās:
He is manifest
In everything
I see.

VI

What is the secret
Of the seed and the tree?
They look so different.

If you can understand the seed,
You will understand
All that is unmanifest.

The branch, the root, the fruit,
The shady leaves,
Are all contained in the seed.

Know
The ultimate Brahma.
Do not think
Of manifest and unmanifest.

He is beyond
The manifest and unmanifest.
Manifest and unmanifest
Are mere names.

A tale that cannot be told,
Beyond all describing.
He who tries to tell this
Is a fool.

Some say
He is in your heart.
That too
Cannot be known.

Great sages, Munis and pundits
They searched for Him,
Charaṇdās, and failed.

'He is manifest,'
'He is unmanifest . . .'
He is neither of these.
However you conceive Him to be,
He is not that either,
No matter how many times you try.

VII

He plays infinite, indivisible,
Endless games
He has infinite qualities
And multiple manifestations.

He takes infinite

Beautiful forms.
Charaṇdās sacrifices himself
To all of them.

The mystery of the Name
Is performed countless times.
Śukdev worships them all.

Rama and Kṛṣṇa complete the circle,
Of twenty-four incarnations.
The formless took these forms
For the sake of his devotees.

VIII

Rag Bilaval

Invisible, Innocent, Infinite, Endless.

The One takes various guises,
Beautiful creations, adorned with jewels.

The formless Hari took different forms,
Immersing Himself in marvelous games.
He watched Himself perform great deeds,
Beheld His own strange wonders.

He was Varaha the boar,
He wrestled with Hiranyaksha,
He rescued the world
From the ocean's depths.

He was a Yaksa and Dattatreya,
Sribadrpati too.
Sanatkumar,

Rsabhadeva and Badhu.

He saved the earth
As a fish and a turtle
Fought a horse, became a lion,
Mahabali the King.

As sage Kapila,
He brought the Ganges
Down from heaven.
Dhavantari, forerunner of a new era.
Parasurama, Ramachandra and Murari.

Three cities rested
In the palm of his hand.
As Kṛṣṇa,
He killed Kamsa the demon.

He was Vedavyasa
And the infamous Buddha.
Twenty-four forms
He assumed in all.

You incarnate
In one age after another;
To overcome evil,
And uphold the saints.

Śukdev told me:
There is neither beginning nor end
To Sham's many stories,
Oh Charaṇdās.

Each story
Is better than the last.

How can we praise you?
You dwell in each palace.

IX

You sit enthroned
In countless dwellings
Rama takes so many forms and shapes
Even Sharada and Ganesha can't count them.

Splendid, beautiful temples,
Wherever I look
My mind is entranced.
Green, white, yellow and red,
Pistachio, purple and black.

Adorned with waving creepers,
Three sided and dappled,
Foursided and spotted,
Decorated by the designer.

How can I describe
All these bright images?
My mind is defeated—
Two legs, four legs . . .

Trees and birds,
Insects and grasshoppers,
Moving and unmoving,
Fish in the sea.
Śukdev explained this to Charaṇdās.

Moving, unmoving,
Changing, unchanging,
Splendid and marvelous in many ways,

Rajas, Tamas, Sattvik,
Some dependent, some not.

Monkey, man, demon, god,
Yaksha spirit, gandharva, ghost,
He lives in all
And loves all equally.

Open the windows of your eyes,
Speak through the door of your mouth.
Tell about Him in many different ways:
Clever and cunning, innocent and wise.

Some people are mute,
Others do not know how to speak.
He is visible in these various palaces—
The visible manifestation of Hari.
Recognize Him.

The field of action
Manifests the atma.
The body is perishable,
The Gita declares,
Only the spirit is immortal.
All you see
Are its coverings.

You revel in the temple of the body;
This is why You are called Ram.
Fortunate are those born into the world.
Śukdev told me this, Charaṇdās.

X

The atma is threaded through everything.

The sun and the ant,
The beginning and the end,
The large and the small.
Nothing is excluded.
There is light in smaller bodies.
And more in the larger.

I will tell the wise
The parable of the lamp.
If they understand my words with love,
Darkness and delusion will be destroyed.

As it is in the body,
So it is in the universe.
Within and without.
Revealed in all seven islands
And nine continents.

Whoever learns this secret
From the True Teacher,
Will look with insight
And see indwelling Brahma.

There is no distinction
Between the knower, knowledge,
And the act of knowing.
There are no differences
Between the meditator, meditation.
And the act of meditation.
When you are one,
The others disappear.
When you are freed from bondage,
There are no more doubts.

Death brings life.

When you are freed from your karma,
Impermanence vanishes.
There is no antagonism,
No punishment for your sins.
Darkness disappears.

Happiness and grief become one.
Some will seek shelter,
Others destroy—
Some will beg for food,
While others give . . .
All will be equal in your eyes,
Your actions are no longer yours.

If you see Hari everywhere,
And nothing as separate from Him,
If you have no desires
That are not His,
You will live in wisdom,
Śukdev told me, Charaṇdās:

It is hard to find wisdom.
Few ever achieve this.
Once you do,
Life and death will be one.

Chapter 7: On Speaking Wisdom

I have seen many speak of wisdom;
I have seldom seen the signs of wisdom.
Lost in their senses, the wise are corrupted,
They say one thing and do another.

With evil karma and malice in their hearts
They forget about virtue and good works.
With sensual lust throbbing in their veins,
They practise lies, deceit and violence.

They cannot restrain their hearts and senses.
They have no fear of sin.
They speak of wisdom but cause dissent.
They know the secret but ignore it.

Brahma's vow is a heavy burden;
Śukdev knew this, Charaṇdās.

When you are fully human,
Not just wise
But established in wisdom,
Then contemplate the Spirit.

Chapter 8: The Nine Aspects of Devotion

Now I sing of devotion,
Which removes the sense of the self.
Charaṇdās says: This is the way
To extinguish the three fires.

I

To master devotion
You must learn its nine aspects:
Hearing, chanting, remembering, serving,
Worship, prostration, obedience, friendship
And self-dedication.

Love the Lord,
Contemplate His feet.
Enjoy the company of the devotees,
Serve them.
This is all that matters.

Once you have offered up your ego,
Remain steadfast,
Forgiving, virtuous,
And contented.
Cling to mercy.

These few words
Are the essence of the Vedas.
They are the root of everything:
Of Yoga, Knowledge and Renunciation.

The splendor of devotion
Destroys these three;
And leaves no room
For duty, wealth, intimacy or liberation,
All who live in the world.

Those who keep
Discernment
And contemplation
In their hearts,
Will attain nirvana
And be saved
From the weight of the world.

Guru Śukdev told me:
Leave illusion.
Serve the feet of the Lord.
Listen with love.

II

Rag Sorath, Gauri or Asavari

Saints, follow the nine aspects
Of devotion.
They are the greatest treasure
Of the Kali Yuga.
If you cling to them,
You will be liberated.

Hear the names of those
Who were jewels in His crown.
I shall tell you their tales
And sing of their deeds.

Prahlad was His servant,
He was saved by contemplation.
Akrur was saved through worship.
Lakshmi lives in His presence,
She serves His lotus feet.

Prithuraja passed over the ocean of existence
Having anointed his body with sandalwood.
King Bali gave his body
And lives at Hari's door forever more.

The supreme devotee, Hanuman,
Was saved by serving Rama.
Sing of Arjuna's greatness—
He was saved through friendship.

King Parikshit was liberated
By listening to the *Bhagavad Purana*.
By hearing Śukdev Muni,
I learned to be like the Lord.

Through the grace of the Guru,
Charaṇdās realized
That loving devotion
Is beyond wisdom, yoga and renunciation.

Chapter 9: Loving Devotion

By practising the nine aspects of devotion
Incomparable love arises.
Rañjīt realized that love
Is the true purpose of life.

Love is the greatest of all teachings,
It is far greater than yoga.
Love gives birth to heroic detachment.
Love feeds renunciation.

Loving devotion shines like the moon,
Dispelling ignorance.
Such love is rare. You cannot buy it.
It is Hari's gracious gift.

The scriptures say that the Lord
Is ruled by love and bliss.
When love awakens in the devotee's heart,
Hari sees its fire burning bright.

The world is created from love alone.
It manifests the unmanifest.
Love is the supreme jewel in the crown.
Charaṇdās is certain of this.

Neither yoga nor knowledge
Equal love.
Without devotion,
Contemplation is useless.

Love liberates us from the world.
Love unites us with Ram.
Love moves in unknowable ways,
And takes us home to Hari.

It turns a crow into a swan.
It makes you one
With the breath of the Beloved.
It takes away your clan, caste and family.
It sows the seeds
Of longing.

If you feel this love for even a moment,
It will destroy all your sins.
When the creeper of love sprouts,
The mind will settle,
Without any yoga.

The skilled musician plays,
Wanting the cup of love.
If you bow down your head,
You will drink deeply at once.

He who is mad in mind and body
Lives in constant contemplation,
And comes close to Hari,
Says Charaṇdās, servant of God.

Hari shines through His lovers,
They never fade.
Guru Śukdev showed me
How to be like this.

Light shines in the eyes
Of a woman in love.

She is filled with affection
And lives at Hari's feet.

Her voice catches in her throat.
Tears fall from her eyes.
Her longing to be with Ram,
Torments her day and night.

Oh! When will I meet Hari?
My heart is breaking.
When will the day come?
When shall I see Him?

Night will not pass
Until I see Him.
My mind will know no peace.
Only Shyam can end my pain.

I cannot live without my Beloved.
The world weighs me down.
If I meet my Darling, I will live,
If I don't, I will die.

My face is pale, lips are cracked.
My eyes dry and forlorn.
My sighs are filled with sorrow,
My breath is shallow and sad.

Separation makes lovers mad.
No one knows how they feel.
Pain burns their heart.
Grief knots their bellies.

She cannot control herself
As she struggles with her loneliness.

Charaṇdās weeps to see her,
Her condition is pitiful.

Words wound the lonely lover,
Gnaw like termites in timber.
They chew day and night
But cannot destroy her heart.

Who understands her?
What has happened to him?
When she remembers him,
A spear pierces her heart.

Whether she wants to or not,
Flooded with passion,
She longs for him,
And lives indifferent
To the whole world.

She weeps during the day
And thinks of him at night.
The separated lover is the perfect disciple,
Devotee, yogi and scholar.

Without Rama, the lover
Has no other friend.
All the day and night
She longs to be with him.

If she sings,
She sings his name.
If she meditates,
She meditates on him.
He is her life.
Her heart is his.

Chapter 10: The Four Great Ages

I

In Satya Yuga, speak the truth,
Worship the Supreme Being,
Uphold the truth,
Never make compromises.
Renounce your body,
But not your breath.
Contemplate Ram:
You will be liberated.
Śukdev told Charaṇdās
The nature of this Age:
Speak the truth, live the truth,
Hold fast to the truth.

II

In the Second Age, worship, veneration,
And love are the way.
There are two ways of worship:
One external, the other internal.
Two types,
One suited to your temperament.
In the end,
Nim's way is best.
Loving devotion
Is the secret of the Second Age.

III

In the Third Age, practice austerity,

Asana and self-discipline,
Restrain your five senses,
Until the mind is subdued.
When the mind is subdued,
The unstruck sound will ring out.
Contemplate your personal deity,
Conquer the self.
This is the way to liberty.
Śukdev showed Charaṇdās
The path of asceticism.

IV

In the Kali Yuga, sing of Hari's virtues,
Morality above all.
Sing loving praises,
Forget fear and doubt.

Forget fear and doubt,
Dissolve caste, clan and pride.
Filled with loving splendor,
Sing of Ram.
This is the only way to be liberated
In the Kali Yuga:
Tell tales of Rama and sing His praise.
Śukdev told Charaṇdās:
Take His hand and cross over.

Chapter 11: A Description of the Name

I honor Śukdev,
Whose teachings are endless.
I sing the greatness of the Name.
O Sādhus, gather around
And hear what I say.

Whatever I say,
I cannot tell the secret.
When you believe in the Name,
Regret disappears.

Birth, death, dying, punishment,
The pain of being in the womb,
When you repeat the Name,
Eighty-four lakh births disappear.

Some perform great sacrifices.
Some concentrate on yoga.
Charaṇdās says: Without the Name,
They are wasting their time.

The philosopher's stone is superior
To the eight base metals.
Ram's Name is beyond austerity,
Pilgrimage, fasting and practice.

The dharma of the greedy
Is like sucking cotton buds.
Action without the Name
Is like winnowing empty husks.

Set aside your desires,
Sit in peace.
Concentrate on His lotus feet.
Remember Ram.

When a Sant does this,
The Creator is pleased.
He reveals Himself
And stays forever.

Vyasa thought deeply and decided
That the essence of the Vedas
Is loving devotion
To the Name of Ram.

He said to Śukdev:
I will tell you how He made
Love renowned throughout the world
In the way that He wanted.

The man who has no love of the Name
Has no fear of evil.
He could murder brahmins,
Women and children.

With the Name in your heart,
You will not suffer in the world.
With the Name in your throat,
Your sins will vanish.
With the Name on your lips,
Everything is yours.

Hari's Name is like this.
It pleases me immensely.

Try it for yourself,
Understand it in your heart.

Even if you don't understand it,
Chanting the Name
Will destroy your sins.
But if you chant with understanding,
You will be liberated
Forever.

When you drink,
Chant the Name.
When you eat,
Chant the Name.
When you sit,
Chant the Name,
When you walk,
Chant the Name.

While you are awake,
Chant the Name.
Focus your mind and body.
Charaṇdās says:
Hari is your friend.

No one else is yours—
Mother, father, son or wife.
Focus your mind on Ram,
Over and over again.

Why have you wandered,
From one house to another?
None of them is yours.
Focus your mind on Ram.

As long as you live,
You will be hungry.
When you die,
Your body will be hungry.
Focus your mind on Ram.
Don't be deceived.

Elephants, horses, great wealth.
Brides with faces like the moon—
If you die without the Name,
You will endure endless suffering.

While you live,
Speak of Ram, love Ram.
Your spirit will come to Ram,
Your body will be left behind.

This is the wonder of the Name,
O Sādhus,
This is the inner essence of devotion.
It is like churning curdled milk
To produce pure ghee.

Chant for eight months
In the mouth,
Chant for sixteen months
In the throat,
Chant for thirty-two months
In your heart.
No sin will remain
In your body.

No sin will remain
In your body,
The seed of devotion

Will sink its deep roots.
The mind will stop;
It will become
A mighty warrior.

Śukdev told Charaṇdās:
This is the secret touchstone,
Return again and again
To the solar plexus.

Chant for five years
At the solar plexus,
Ram will be in your every vein.
The body and spirit
Of my own devotee
Will come to Ram's abode.

Chant the Name of Ram
At the eyebrow center,
The light will shine.
Chant with your breath,
Duality will fade.

Chant at the top of your skull,
Where the sky opens wide.
In this way, says Charaṇdās,
You will enter Hari's court.

Focus on the tip of your nose
And you will see light shining.
Charaṇdās says: There are still more wonders
To be seen, O Sādhus.

Raise the Name
From the solar plexus

Into the sky,
You will see that light.
Śukdev taught me this.

Chant in your heart of hearts,
The mirror will shine.
You will see Ram.
All darkness will disappear.

Chant the Name softly.
The seven psychic centers
And five senses
Will vanish,
And the mind will settle.
Charaṇdās says:
This is true.

The mind of those who chant in contemplation,
Will not be bound by the body.
They will merge with Sat-cit-ananda
And live surrounded by silence.

The Name is the crest jewel,
The highest religion of all.
Those who know devotion
Will always be mindful.

They will not believe in other religions,
They will not meditate on other gods.
Anyone who finds true devotion
Will understand this.

II

A faithful wife obeys her husband,

She always fulfils his commands.
She enjoys his love
And is distracted by no other man.

She serves her beloved
And ignores other men's bodies.
She is content with her own house
And indifferent to other dwellings.

She obeys her beloved
And is faithful to him.
She serves him completely
And loves no one else.

She gives her love to her beloved,
Other men are poison.
Her house is filled with sunshine,
Other houses are filled with darkness.

She would rather suffer in her own house
Than know pleasure somewhere else.
This is the way of the good wife,
The faithful woman.

She gazes upon her husband
And has no interest in other men.
She chants Hari's Name
And forgets all other gods.

Ram is your beloved,
Do not seek another.
Charaṇdās says:
This is how you should think.

If you bow your head,

Bow only to Ram.
Otherwise, do not bow at all.
Do not be tempted by other gods,
Even if it costs your life.

The faithful wife keeps her vows.
She would never betray her husband.
Marriage destroys her suffering
And provides endless happiness.

When you recognize the Beloved,
He will make you his own.
You will sit in a place of honor,
He will make you happy.

This is my teaching.
Hold it close to your heart.
Sow a mighty seed
And you can sit in its shade.

The honest man speaks the truth,
You can trust his words.
He holds Hari's Name in one hand
And weighs the world in the other.

I speak the essence
Of untainted devotion.
Saying Ram's Name aloud
Equals a million acts of penance.

Speak Ram's Name with your mouth,
Hear Ram's Name with your ears.
Drown yourself in Hari.
Cling to the hem of His clothing.

Wisdom contains many doctrines,
Austerity holds great wealth.
Yoga will make you perfect,
But Ram's Name will liberate you.

Renounce all desires,
Cling to Ram's Name.
You will overcome obstacles
And reach Hari's home.

Ram's Name covers everything:
Wealth, perfection, liberation.
Set your sights on such a Lord.
This is what Charaṇdās teaches.

He made everything:
The seven continents
And the nine realms.
This is what Charaṇdās says,
The three worlds
And the whole universe.

He does everything for you.
He makes you happy
In so many ways.
You cannot know him
If you do not take His Name.

You have been born
In a human form,
You can praise Him.
This is what Charaṇdās says:
Take Ram's Name.

III

Rag Kedara

Listen to the power of the Name,
My brothers.
It contains liberation, the four perfections,
And the eight precious elements.
Valmiki lived in the forest
He was a sinner
But he became great
By accidentally chanting the Name
Backwards.

The courtesan was a great sinner;
She went to Hari's city
Through the power of the Name.
Fallen Ajamil lived with a prostitute,
He went to Hari's city,
Mounted on a chariot,
By calling the name of his son.

Countless other sinners were saved,
How can I tell of them all?
The Name is greater
Than giving alms, reciting mantras,
Austerity, yoga, or self-control.

Vyasa, Narada, Shiva, Shesa the serpent,
Brahma and his sons,
All chant Ram's Name.
Śukdev taught Charaṇdās
The power of the Name.

IV

Kavita

Through the power of the Name,
Nandalal became the Lord.
Through the power of the Name,
The son was called Dasaratha.
Through the power of the Name,
Prahlad's honor was saved.
Through the power of the Name,
Arjuna announced the destruction of Dvaraka.

I cannot express
The power of the Name.
The saints praise
The power of the Name
Charaṇdās has placed his trust
In the power of the Name
The Vedas proclaim:
The name is pure!
Pure!

Through the power of the Name,
Sabari turned wine into water.
Through the power of the Name,
Adhama came into the world.
Through the power of the Name,
The chariot came for Ajamil.
Through the power of the Name,
The elephant was saved
From the alligator's jaws.

Through the power of the Name,
Suffering is vanquished.

Through the power of the Name,
Śukdev was manifested.
Charaṇdās lives
Through the power of the Name.
All four Vedas say:
The Name is pure!
Pure!

I have said all I can
On the power of the Name.
Now I will tell you
About the five ghosts.
So please listen carefully.

Chapter 12: The Five Hungry Ghosts

These five hungry ghosts
Will ruin yoga,
Austerity and devotion.
While you live,
You will suffer in the world.
When you die,
You will burn in hell.

Lust, anger, delusion, greed,
The fifth is pride.
They rule the world
And poison everyone.

How can I describe
The army of lust
Which overwhelms the brave?
Woman is the paymaster,
Who conquers the great
And the virtuous.

I On Lust

Rag Soratha

Women are powerful, O Sādhus.
Why not praise Ram instead?
Women can destroy a man's love
And make him dance

Like a monkey on a chain.

Eyes circled with mascara
Make it easy to forget
Mercy and morality.
A glance can steal your heart
Even though the world mock you.

You are willing to give up everything
For her sake.
But in the end
You will hold your head in your hands
And weep.

The treasure of human birth
Will waste away,
Black lines cover the face.
Time passes quickly.
The soul is born
Again and again.

Skilled in the tactics of desire,
She is a consummate lover.
Woman slays the greatest warriors,
The bravest of men.

Guru Śukdev told me:
I will show you the dacoit.
Charaṇdās, you must recognize
The ways of deception.

At the sight of a woman,
A man forgets everything.
King or commoner,
Shaven or shriven,

Flirtatious eyes
Entrance all alike.

Desire, a red sari, a sly walk.
Adorned with jewellery
And eye shadow.
A smiling face,
Sweet words,
Bind the saint
In desire and pleasure.

Many have abandoned yoga,
Many have renounced austerities,
Many have lost their devotion,
For the sake of sensual embraces.

Making merry, dancing many dances,
Capture a man in desire.
Be careful of this, Sādhus,
Understand me well.

Guru Śukdev told me:
Recognize the thief.
Charaṇdās admits this is hard,
But there is something better.

Sādhus, beware
Of other men's wives.
If you see them and touch them
In this life,
You will live in hell in the next.

Indra left his throne
When he heard of Gautam's beautiful wife.
Everyone knows what happened to him

And the shame he endured.

The gods were frightened,
Seeing the sage Srngi practising austerities
In the forest.
They sent Rambha to defeat him
And he was lost at once.

All the gods, every man,
Have been bewitched by women.
I will tell you today
The consequences of their actions.

Śukdev taught me:
You will never be saved—
Saint or sinner—
When you dance in the embrace of love.

Do not stare
At other men's wives.
If you stare at a witch
She will eat you alive.

The sap of the *ak* tree
Burns like a fire;
Its poison can kill a lion,
Passion can destroy a man

Hell's mines are painful.
You will wander
In 84 lakh births.
From one life to another
You will be cursed.
Hari is the only guru
Who can save you.

With body and mind polluted,
You will wander
Without honor.
Śukdev advised me, Charaṇdās,
Ram is beautiful.

Men and women beware!
I have made it clear.
If you enjoy
Other people's partners,
You will go to hell.

Another man's wife
Is good and bad.
She is a fire outside your house.
She will burn your hand
If you touch her.

I—2 How to Conquer Lust

Stop flirting.
Stop arguing
About who is most attractive.
Do not be entranced by good looks.
Be nobody's lover.

There is a bright shield
Which can protect you
From passion.
Love's army has eight wings.
Ignore them all.

Firstly, desire enters

The ears.
Then it enters
The eyes.
Finally, it invades
Your heart.
It makes you suffer.

Brother, love is bad.
It drives your body mad.
You will be shamed in public
And beaten with shoes.

You will be a public spectacle,
Black faced, riding an ass.
Reviled like a wandering dog,
Everyone will think you a fool.

No one will speak to your face.
You will wander the world in shame,
Alive, but living in hell.
Hear and beware,
Men and women.

Abandon the path of passion,
Cling to the company of the pure.
Charaṇdās says: Make your home
With Hari's devotees.

Passion scorches the heart and body,
It drives the mind wild.
It destroys karma and dharma
And makes you forget
Everything else.

Desire strikes down

Compassion and forgiveness.
It overthrows effort and truth,
It distracts you completely.

Passion destroys
Pure spiritual practices.
It throws dust in your face,
It denies you fame.
Desire weaves a garland of sins.

It makes patience impossible,
It makes you tell lies.
Your actions are confused,
Your mind is fixed
On sensual pleasure.

When Kama's army arrives,
It brings many faults.
Kamadeva is full of faults,
Few can conquer him.

Sādhus! The devotee
Who conquers this scoundrel
Is a virtuous person.
Beware! said Śukdev.
Charaṇdās listened carefully.

Listen to what I say.
Pay heed and obey.
Grasp the sword of virtue
And destroy passion!

II On Anger

Everybody knows

Anger is the lowest of the low.
Listen carefully
As I describe its nature.

I will tell of the hungry ghost
Named Anger.

It assumes many forms.
When it possesses your mind and body
All awareness is lost.
Red eyes, black body,
Every vein filled with murder.

The untouchable Anger
Is base and dreadful.
She overturns good sense.
You will beat yourself
And tear your clothes,

Froth at the mouth, babble,
Shout insults,
And wring your hands.
Huff and puff,
Curse yourself,
Throw your plate away
Instead of eating.

Sometimes you take up weapons,
At other times, you run and hide.
If someone praises you,
You will insult them.
Praise or insult,
You will respond
By throwing rocks.

You are meek,
In the presence of the strong.
And bold,
In the presence of the weak.
Śukdev told Charaṇdās:
An angry man does
Whatever he wants.

Whatever form Anger assumes,
It rushes at you
And knocks you flat.
It destroys your faith
And twists your mind,
Whether you be man or woman.

Anger knocks down reason,
And hits you
Again and again.
It fills the body with violence,
Leaving no room
For compassion.

The angry man
Insults the Guru.
The angry man
Pokes fun at Sādhus.
The angry man
Takes away your love for Hari.
The angry man
Pulls you down to hell.

The angry man
Is treacherous.
The angry man
Is a fool.

The angry man
Never goes unpunished.
In the end,
He will lose his head.

Never speak to an angry person,
Be afraid of their ways.
Never let Anger come near you.
Never forgive or embrace it.

When you pardon an angry person
And make room for them,
Their anger will be defeated.
Guru Śukdev said:
Listen, Charaṇdās,
Be skilful
And free others from harm.

This completes the chapter on Anger,
Now I will turn to Delusion,
Which brings great suffering
And never leaves you alone.

III On Delusion

Delusion and Infatuation
Spread their nets
And carry sharp spears.
They attack and capture
Many men and women.

We know from experience
That affection leads
To delusion.
Charaṇdās tells you:

Repentance is useless.

Like a deer caught in a trap,
You will jump
And try to break free,
But you cannot.
Things will only get worse.

Delusion is the honey
For which the fly risks its life.
Caught in the grip of infatuation,
It loses its head.

Your home is your prison,
Each day you are beaten
And burned.
Infatuation will separate you from Ram
And cast you down into hell.

You will wander
Through 84 lakh births.
Even if you have a chance to escape,
You will never be free.

The worst delusion
Is infatuation with women.
Infatuation with your children
Brings nothing but pain.
Infatuation with your family,
Brother and relatives,
Will make you blind,
You fool.

Gods and ghosts run to and fro,
For the sake of their families.

Tricksters, thieves,
Deceitful businessmen,
Clothes, jewellery,
Fine carriages—
All of these
Attack your spirit.

Money and rubies,
Diamonds and pearls,
Fascinate the foolish.
Home, land and village,
Endlessly dazzle you.
But the greatest fascination
Is with your own name.

Kings and paupers suffer equally.
Everyone knows
The pain it brings.
You are in anguish
Because of other people's actions.
You will lose
Everything you own.

The greatest sorrow comes
When you forget
To contemplate Ram.
Few conquer Infatuation.

Śukdev told Charaṇdās:
The man who meets Ram
Is a true Sādhu.
He will be liberated
And freed from this world.

III—2 Escaping Delusion

Infatuation brings the greatest suffering.
Conquer it and escape.
Renounce your love of the world
And you will be free from desire.

Live in the world,
The way the tongue
Lives in the mouth.
You can eat thick ghee,
And not be greasy.

Live in the world,
Like the lotus in a lake.
You can feed on the water
And escape the mud.

If you can live like that,
You will be a true Sādhu,
Freed from attachment.
If you worship
The lotus feet of the Lord,
You will be untouched
By worldly desires.

Infatuation's army
Is powerful beyond description.
It has conquered
The whole world,
It makes everyone mad.

IV On Greed

I will describe vile Greed,
The source of great sin;

Whose minister is a liar,
A completely dishonest man.

His wife is Desire,
She will make you blind,
You will lose
Everything you own.
Don't you understand?
Aren't you afraid of Death?

Greed is the companion
Of the proud and deceitful
Crocodile,
Which will carry you off to hell
After you die,
And drive you crazy
While you are still alive.

Greed
Makes you forget dharma,
Leads you towards immorality,
Turns you from Hari,
Fills you with evil desires.

Greed
Makes you wander
Through the four countries,
With strife and false awareness
As your companions.
It will reach out and strike you
Even in shady groves.

Sādhus and the Puranas all say:
A true devotee
Can never be greedy.

The greedy widow
Won't be a warrior;
The greedy donor
Won't be a saint.

The greedy supporter
Won't be faithful;
The greedy person
Loves the world.

Greedy men and women
Live for money;
Even when they die,
They cling to their bodies.

Greedy men and women
Injure living creatures;
Greedy people
Are always deceitful.

Greedy men and women
Are not afraid of sin;
Greedy people
Suffer continually.

Greedy men and women
Would sell their own heads;
Greedy people
Drown in sensuality.

Guru Śukdev
Told me this.
Charaṇdās says:
Don't be greedy,

Place your trust
In Hari's protection.

Greedy ants, monkeys and vultures,
All suffer greatly.
Choose Hari,
Renounce Greed.
Charaṇdās praises
Wise men and women.

Greed consumes honor,
Makes you depend on the world.
Greed creates burdens, causes loss,
Leads to impurity,
Drives away discernment.

When Greed goes,
Satisfaction
Takes its place.
This great army brings its allies:
Renunciation and truth
And drives away
Discord and sorrow.

Contentment
Fills the whole body;
Worldly pleasure never will.
Pleasure that stretches
From here to heaven
Will only make you sick.

When you contemplate Ram,
True contentment rules.
Don't stop meditating,
Don't run here and there.

Don't desire anything,
Don't wish to be somewhere else.
Be completely content,
Have no cares.

Hari's servants
Have no desire for the world.
Charaṇdās says that the sick
Cannot be saved.

Here follows the chapter on Pride.

V On Pride

I have written four chapters,
Now I will tell you
About Pride.

Great emperors have wandered
Sheltered by parasols;
Pride led them
Into sensual lives.
Souls have wandered
Through 84 lakh births.
Why don't you try to escape?

Blinded by Pride, men have lost
Their wives and their fortunes.
Had they been free of self-regard
They would have reached Hari's court.

Charaṇdās says:
As long as egoism survives,
You must deal

With these five vices.
You must endure the flames of the world
As long as self-regard and conceit
Remain in your heart.

If you are constantly conceited,
Deceitful, dishonest and cunning,
You will wander around,
Like a ghost in a graveyard.

The proud can never be liberated;
They will lose all their senses.
They put on such airs and graces,
But no one is less worthy than they.

To be happy, you must be humble,
Especially if you seek true bliss.
The proud play with lies and deceptions,
Pretending clay pots are golden chalices.
With deceit and hypocrisy always in mind,
They never come close to the truth.

They wander around saying "I," "I," "I,"
And have no respect for others.
In life, these are the symptoms of their pain.
In death, such traits lead to hell.

Charaṇdās says:
Listen, wise saints.
The source of liberation
Is Meekness;
The source of hell
Is Pride.

The beautiful become proud

And ignore the innocent.
The youthful are proud,
And run wild in the dark.

The proud say: I am rich,
That makes me wise and powerful.
The proud say: my family is pure.
We belong to the topmost caste.

The proud boast of their learning;
They argue like fools.
Kings boast of their strength,
Thinking only of themselves.

Monarchs ignore death.
They grow fat on other men's corpses.
One day they'll die,
Then they'll know true suffering.
Guru Śukdev warned me:
See what is in front of you.

When a man says proudly, I'm fine,
He is boasting.
At that very moment,
He may be thrown into hell.

Awaken, oh men and women,
Renounce intoxication,
Forget your jealousy
Take shelter at the feet of Sādhus.

If you devoutly contemplate Ram,
All your sicknesses will disappear.
Renounce caste, life-stage and family,
Immerse yourself in satsang.

Once you are liberated,
You will never be born again.
Guru Śukdev said: Charaṇdās,
Keep these things
Close to your heart.

Practise interior contemplation,
Remove all your pride.
When you are humble,
All other shortcomings
Will fade away.

Once these five ghosts have fled,
You will become
Pure Spirit.
You will know true bliss.
Every thing you see
Will be the embodiment
Of perfect freedom.

Through the power of the True Guru,
I have sung
Of the five ghosts.
Now I will speak
Of virtue,
Which erases sin.

Here ends my description
Of the five hungry ghosts.

Chapter 13
How to Ward off the Five Hungry Ghosts

I A Chapter on Virtue

Now I will sing of virtue,
The way of the wise saint.
Listen to me, men and women,
Pay attention to what I say.

You may be beautiful, decent,
Noble and wealthy,
But if you do not practise
True morality,
You will be polluted
And fall into hell.

The immoral
Who practise austerity,
The immoral
Who give alms,
The immoral
Who practise yoga,
Are all fools.

Virtue
Is the greatest yoga.
Without morality,
Liberation is impossible.

You may have many good qualities,
But unless they are based

On true virtue,
They will count for nothing.
Chanting and austerities
Will bear no fruit.
This is my teaching.

Worship, self-discipline, vows,
The careful offering of sacrifices,
Charaṇdās says: Without true virtue,
Will be of no benefit.

There are widows who are great warriors,
There are generous donors,
They are constant
In their practise of virtue,
None of their actions
Is wasted.

Virtue is superior
To all twenty-nine qualities.
The body
Not governed by virtue
Is base.

You can't grow virtue
In the ground;
You can't buy virtue
In the market-place.
If you rely on virtue,
It will support you
Completely.

Without virtue,
You will fall into hell.
Without virtue,

Death will be painful.
Without virtue,
You'll wander
Through seven continents
And nine lands.

Without virtue,
You'll wander
Through 84 lakh births,
You will assume the form
Of a ghost.
This is certain.

Abandon everything else
For the sake of virtue.
Concentrate on the Name of Ram.
You will live with honor
In this world;
You will be liberated
When you die.

The truly virtuous person,
The truly great man,
Will be honored
In this world.
Hear what I say.

Nothing important is lost
While virtue remains.
A king is always safe,
When he has his army.

If truth is lost,
Something may be left.
If virtue is lost,

Nothing remains.
If the fence is broken,
The field will be at risk.

An immoral youth
Will destroy the body.
Nothing will come from repentance
But further shame.

An immoral man
Receives no honour.
He lives in the world
Like a stray dog,
Abused and despised
Wherever he goes.

If you lose virtue,
You will lose the Guru,
And turn away from Hari.
Charaṇdās says:
How many times must I tell you,
You will lose everything.

Those who abandon virtue
Will live wretched lives.
Born again and again,
Suffer cruel deaths.

Virtue is like sour tamarind,
It adds flavour to the dish
And greatness to your life.
Charaṇdās says:
Taste and see.

Virtue is like a healing lime.

It strengthens the body.
At first,
It may seem sour,
But it will make you happy.

Drinking the water
Used to wash the feet
Of virtuous persons
Will cure your body and soul,
And save you
From the fear of death.

Charaṇdās says:
It is a rare sight
To see a man whose whole body
Glows with true virtue.

The sight of a virtuous man
Is magnificent;
It destroys sin,
Purifies the mind,
And corrects your vision.

Bathe in the lake
Of virtue.
Śukdev said:
It is the best
Of all pilgrim sites.

This completes
The chapter on virtue.
The importance of this topic
Is beyond compare.
Now I will describe compassion,
Understand this and live

A balanced life.

II On Compassion

The greatest goal in life
Is compassion.
Love removes enmity
And destroys the bonds
Of karma.

Love everything in the world:
Things that move,
And those that don't.
Give the gift
Of compassion.

Eat with awareness.
Drink filtered water.
Do not cut growing trees.
These methods will help you
Avoid bad karma.

Many people have considered
The nature of karma.
Compassion
Is the greatest austerity,
It is true religion.

Avoid violence.
Do not seek to hurt
Creatures with one sense,
Two, three, four,
Or even five.

Eat with awareness.

Sit carefully.
Whatever you do,
Act with understanding.
This is the way to live.

Be at peace
In your thinking.
Be sweet
In your speech.
May your actions
Serve life.
Charaṇdās says this
To all who will listen.

Don't speak harshly,
Cause no harm,
Treat other people
As one with yourself,
Hari will take away
Your suffering.

Those who speak harsh words,
Who hurt others by their actions,
Are violent people,
Eager to destroy
Compassion
And true religion.

Be mindful, understanding,
Use your five senses
And five means of action,
Adding the eleventh—
Your mind.
Do good to all.
Charaṇdās says:

Understand this.

Do not hurt anything,
Friend or foe.
Benefit the world.
Practise compassion
At all times.

Be gentle.
Sympathize with those who suffer.
Be noble.
Be innocent.
These aspects of compassion
Will liberate you.

Compassion brings wisdom.
Compassion leads to devotion.
Charaṇdās says: Compassion will take you
To the Beloved.

If there is no compassion,
There is nothing.
Your words will be empty.
There will be sweetness on your lips,
And bitterness in your heart.

False Sādhus wear marks
On their foreheads,
And carry rosaries
In their hands,
They are like deceitful cranes
Waiting to strike.

With hard hearts
And no compassion,

They live in a city
Filled with violence
And deceit.

How can you be a wise pundit,
If you have no compassion
For living beings?
How can you churn knowledge
And fail to distill
True compassion?

What can I say, pundit?
Are you a wise man
Or a fool?
Are you a sieve,
Or a winnowing fan?

True compassion destroys sin,
Pain, suffering and conflict.
Only a blind fool would abandon
This supreme virtue.

Without compassion,
You're a fallen creature.
Without compassion,
You're corrupted.
Without compassion,
You may listen
But your words will be empty.

You won't escape
Birth and death.
You won't escape
The consequences of your actions.
Without compassion,

You'll receive your just reward,
In all 84 lakh births.

Charaṇdās says:
When compassion arises,
Lust, anger, delusion,
Greed and pride,
Are destroyed.

Charaṇdās says:
When compassion arises,
No matter how many enemies you have,
No one will want to hurt you.

Removing harm, helping others,
This is the way to govern
The city of your body.
The bandit queen and her thieves
Will quickly flee.

Blessed morality!
Blessed compassion!
These please Ram.
Guru Śukdev told me:
They fulfill your desires.

Here ends my description
Of the way to ward off
The five hungry ghosts.

Chapter 14: The Manifestation of Maya

I

The true disciples live
In the presence of the Guru.
They are content
To pass the night
Alone.

They please Ram
By their loving kindness.
Their speech is moderate,
Their teaching considered.
They do not argue
With idle debaters.

They maintain silence,
And seldom speak.
They keep unblinking vigils
Throughout the night.
They fix their gaze
At the tip of their noses.
When they do speak,
Their words are sweet
And true.

In meditation,
The true disciples
Turn back their tongues
And ascend into the sky.
There are no clouds

But a gentle rain falls.
By cultivating their breath
They stabilize their emotions.
They are not tempted
By wealth or sensual pleasures.

Disciples who sit in silence,
Mindful of the unstruck sound,
With heart open,
Separate from the world,
Are great men and women.
Śukdev told me this.

When the disciples speak,
They speak of Ram.
When they are silent,
They meditate.
Those who follow these practices,
Says Charaṇdās,
Are wise.

II

I will tell of the greatness
Of maya, illusion,
Which shapes samsara,
Suffering.
Maya forms an unfolding drama,
Splendid, incomprehensible,
Endless.

Everything manifest
Is maya.
Everything that has color,
That changes its shape and forms,

Is fickle,
An unreal delusion.

Like a dream in the night,
Like a face in a mirror,
Maya is visible but non-existent,
Like the shadow of a tree.

Maya fascinates us all.
Those who long for the world
Are under its spell.

It is so bewitching,
We drown in its glow.
It glitters and sparkles,
Assumes diverse forms:
Sometimes a pauper,
And sometimes a king.

Countless dramas are played out,
Everywhere,
In all manner of forms:
Lust, anger, jealousy, greed,
Pride and arrogance,
The concern for status.

Everything the five senses recognize
Is a manifestation of maya.
The five elements and the three gunas
Are all forms of maya.

Maya smiles temptingly,
Like a crocodile.
Taking endless forms,
Hour after hour.

Śukdev made me understand
All of maya's games.

All the pleasures of the world
Are shrouded in maya.
There are two aspects to illusion:
One is money,
The other sensual pleasure.

Greed and desire come together;
They destroy many people.
We focus on ourselves
And not on liberation.

Whatever the five senses see
Are aspects of maya.
Everything with form
Is a manifestation of maya.

Maya assumes countless forms.
Sādhus and saints know this.
Whatever you speak of,
Hear and see,
They are all forms of maya.

Yogis and ascetics are deluded
By the eight perfections
And the nine treasures—
These too are forms of maya.
All human beings are trapped
In maya's snare.

They will suffer in hell.
They will witness
Death's fifty-six torments.

They will be reborn
Eighty four lakh times,
From one womb to another.

They will wander the world
Shaped like animals.
They will never find liberation.
Charaṇdās says: Awake, oh mankind!
You will never benefit
Unless you abandon maya.

Renounce all desire for the world.
Do not be entranced by maya.
Live free from karma.
Be the embodiment
Of perfect freedom.

Chapter 15: The Mind

Don't be trapped by sense objects,
Meditate on the lotus feet of the Master.
Desire nothing else.
Avoid maya's arrows.

Wisdom is great,
Meditation is even greater.
Through meditation,
You will meet the Beloved,
You will find nirvana.

Mediation brings the meditator
And the object of meditation
Together.
Three must merge into one,
If you are to find nirvana.

If the mind is controlled by the senses,
The senses will control your awareness.
Tell me:
As long as duality remains,
How can there be true meditation?

Where the senses go,
The mind goes with them,
And so does your awareness.
This is certain.

Where the mind and senses go,
Awareness goes with them.

Charaṇdās says:
Understand this,
If you want to succeed.

Use your mind
To control your senses;
Unify your mind and awareness.
Place your awareness
On Hari.
Meditate continually on Him.

When the mind and senses merge,
Sensual desires arise;
In the same way that
When a man and a woman meet
Their passions are kindled.

When the components are separate,
Nothing happens.
Oh Sādhus!
Keep the mind and the senses
Separate.
This is Śukdev's way.

Keep the mind separate
From the senses.
Perfect mindfulness
Through non attachment—
Through the stilling
Of sensual desires.
This is the way to enlightenment,
Oh Charaṇdās.

Control your senses.
If you do not,

Your fickle mind
Will drink deep
Of sensual delight.

Once the senses taste delight,
You will never be able
To control your mind.
The mind will shift and change,
No matter what you do;
Even if you try
A hundred thousand times.

Each and every sense
Has its own object of delight.
There is no disputing this:
There are five senses,
Each with its object.

Unless you can smash these enemies,
You will never be victorious.
I have thought deeply about this;
There is no other way.

I will speak about each of the five,
And tell you their secrets.
If you can conquer them all,
You will never know sorrow.

I The Sense of Sight

Consider the sense of sight.
It causes great pain and suffering.
It leads to both hate and love,
Elation and grief.

It entangles us in forms,
Damages mind and body.
It makes you a slave to other people,
It can destroy your family.

It can catch you in a noose,
Burn you with desire.
It flickers
And sends you into a frenzy.
It can weaken your resolve
And drive you crazy.

A Sādhu or warrior turns away;
They avert their eyes
From the world.
Charaṇdās says: listen to me,
Live like the tortoise.

Fascinated by the lamp,
The moth falls into the flame,
Losing everything,
Including its life.

The sense of sight
Consumes mind and body.
When the path of Ram is lost,
Sensual desires grow stronger.

How can you be liberated
When you have no respect for life?
Why lament your fate,
When this trouble
Is your own fault?

The sense of sight is an enemy

Which destroys mindfulness.
It creates attachment to maya,
And makes you wander
In 84 lakh births.

It removes all modesty
And sows the seeds
Of stupidity.
It is a trickster's chatter
And the spark
Which ignites the karma
That can destroy you.

It removes your merit.
It shows you
The sufferings of hell.
Guru Śukdev told me:
The eyes
Cause great suffering.

What you see
Is not your own.
Guru Śukdev said:
Listen carefully,
Charaṇdās.

Gaze upon Sādhus
Who serve their Guru well.
See Brahma wherever you look,
Abandon duality
And malice.

When you see
Your enemy and friend
In the same way—

The ugly and the beautiful
In the same way—
Then your mind has control
Over your senses.

II The Sense of Hearing

Listen as I speak
Of the second sense,
Through the grace of the Guru.
The mind is lost when it hears
Sentimental love songs.
Waves of desire arise
And ruin your meditation.

When you hear tales of greed,
Your head fills with plans.
Should you become rich,
You will worry
How to keep your wealth.

Whether you have stolen money,
Tricked others,
Or found hidden treasure,
However you gained it,
Wealth will always
Make you weep.
Greed is like the cauliflower
Growing into a great sin.

Charaṇdās says: I have thought about this.
Wake up, men and women!
Wake up!

II—I Hearing and Pride in One's Family

Now listen while I discuss
Pride in your family,
Which leads to arrogance
And contempt for others.
When you tell how important you are,
You strengthen your sense of self.
You bark about yourself
Like a dog
Disturbed from its sleep.
When pride increases,
Modesty and humility vanish.
You enjoy criticizing others,
You hate hearing them praised.
When arrogance overwhelms your mind,
Humility vanishes,
And there can be no liberation.
Listening encourages arrogance
And leads to arguments.
When your mind is filled with anger,
You want to hurt your rival.
When you hear the sweet music of the flute,
You are happy, sad,
Or distressed.
When you hear of something good
Your family has done,
You are happy.
When you hear of a problem
In your family,
You weep.
The hunter tricks the deer
By playing sweet music,
Then kills it with an arrow.

Śukdev said: Listen and learn,
These are the faults
Of wrong listening.

II—2 Right Listening

With your mind,
Listen to stories of Hari.
With your ears,
Hear of Hari's fame.

If you can contemplate in this way,
You will be a wise devotee.
The wise devotees know union,
They are yoked with Ram.

In undivided love,
Joy arises,
And the desire to see Ram.

By hearing,
One becomes a Sādhu.
By hearing,
You know
The unknowable secret.

Hearing encourages you
To serve Sants and Sādhus.
If you listen to the Guru,
You will need no other.

By listening,
Awe and modesty arise;
All your works
Will turn out well.

By listening,
One becomes a Sant,
A seer;
One becomes humble,
And loses all pride.

By listening,
You cease to be afraid
Of death.
You will no longer suffer
The 84 lakh births.

By listening,
You will find
The four treasures;
You will burn the seeds
Of endless rebirth.

By listening,
The crow became a swan.
Śukdev told me this.

By right listening,
True awareness arises;
One is absorbed
In Hari's love.
By wrong listening
False awareness arises;
The waves of emotion
Are futile.

The sense of hearing
Has a double nature.
It is worth every effort

To hear stories of Kṛṣṇa
And the songs that praise Him;
The words of the Guru and Sādhus
Will change you completely;
They will lead you away
From sensual delights
And bring you to Hari.

III The Sense of Taste

I have spoken about listening
In both its forms;
Charaṇdās says: Please hear
What I say
About taste.

Taste will trick you.
It longs to experience
The six flavors of food.
It can make you ill
And spoil your life.

Taste is the great devourer,
Be afraid of gluttony.
Taste tempts you to steal,
It steals you in turn.
Taste can burn you
And make you poor.
It leads to wrong actions,
And your humiliation.
It confuses you in lies.
Friend! It can lead you to hell.
If you gamble with gluttony,
People will despise you.
Each of the five vices

Is shaped by greed.
Know this and be strong,
Says Rañjīt.
Unless you conquer greed,
Your whole life will be wasted.
Charaṇdās says: In this world,
Your life will be wretched.

To catch a fish,
You drop a line into a pond.
Its greed makes the fish
Suffer and die.

The sense of taste
Is a heavy burden;
Whoever does not renounce it
Is a very big fool.

Take Hari's Name,
Chew on His virtues
And teachings,
Put nothing else into your mouth.

Speak sweet words,
Be humble.
Think first
Before you open your mouth.

Eat plain food,
For Ram's sake.
Charaṇdās says: This is the way
The warrior wins.

If you can subdue your tongue,
You will conquer

Your whole body.
Guru Śukdev says:
Enjoy the fruits
Of liberation.

The devotee who conquers taste
Is a true yogi, true Sādhu,
Who finds the invisible path
To the unreachable land.

IV The Sense of Touch

Touch is passion's plaything,
It constantly offers new games.
Animals, birds, demons and men,
Are all caught in its longings.

Pleasure is found
In soft caresses
And gentle strokes,
Dark eyes adorned with black.
It is found
In oils and garlands,
The supple swaying of a body.

Pleasure is found
In clothing and jewellery;
In adornment and decoration.
It is found
In knowing how and where to touch.

When it traps you both,
How can you escape?
You are caught in knots
Confirmed by affectionate words.

New obstacles will appear
One after the other—
Beyond your comprehension.
It will be too late to repent;
You will be led away,
Down to hell.

Charaṇdās says:
Don't you realize?
Can't you see
Your errors?

Everyone is ruled
By the skin's sweet touch.
All are caught
In the snares of the world.
Everyone wants to escape,
But no one can.

The female elephant is used
To trap the rogue male.
Though he regrets his foolishness,
He cannot escape the ditch.

Through the grace of Kamadev,
The mahout raises his prod
And rules the beast.
The rogue elephant
Sported in the forest;
Now he is tied with a rope
And comes to your door.

Like the elephant,
A man can be bound

By the form of a girl.
He will suffer
For the rest of his life.
He will be caught
In the deep well
Of ignorance.

He will not worship Hari,
He will not serve the Guru.
He will not sing Hari's praises,
He will not share in satsang.

It will happen again,
When he is next reborn.
Eighty-four lakh times,
He will do it all again.

To conquer the sense of touch,
Śukdev said,
You should practise austerity,
Hear me, Charaṇdās.

Ignore the pain of hot and cold,
Think of hard and soft as one.
Spend your life
In the practice of austerity.
Avoid the eight perfumes.

Stay away from skin.
Don't let passion's fires
Burn in your heart.
The body is your forest.
Practise austerity
In your heart.

I have told you the secret,
The way to conquer touch.
Guru Śukdev told me:
Use the body
To practise austerity.

If you can conquer touch,
You can defeat passion.
If you practise austerity, truth,
Morality and contentment,
You will escape maya's grip.

V The Sense of Smell

Now I have talked about touch,
I will speak of the sense of smell.
I will tell you the story
Of the bee and the elephant.

Attracted by a sweet fragrance
A honeybee settled on a lotus.
When a cloud passed, the petals closed,
And the bee struggled, unable to escape.

An elephant came
Down to the lake
To drink some water
And play about.

The elephant picked the lotus
And twirled it
Above his head,
Then he smashed it down
And broke it to pieces.

A man is caught
In the same way,
Says Charaṇdās,
And enters
The jaws of death.

Treat a sweet smell
And a foul stench
As the same.
If you can do this,
You will conquer
The sense of smell,
And still the buzzing of the mind.

There is one way to understand this
And a thousand ways to forget.
The senses tell of virtue and vice,
The mind calls for awareness.

If you are ruled by the senses,
You will be bound
And taken to hell,
You will wander
In 84 lakh births
And suffer continually in the womb.

Those who are ruled by the senses
Will never find bliss.
They will cling to the same relationships
Over and over again.

They will never know devotion
And their works will all come to grief.
Those who are ruled by the senses
Will never meet Ram.

Charaṇdās says: Having resolved
To conquer the senses,
Forget the world, find Hari,
And enter the state of nirvana.

By conquering the senses,
One becomes a knower of Brahma.
By conquering the senses,
One becomes a meditator.
By conquering the senses,
One becomes a servant of Hari,
Dwelling in an immortal realm.
By conquering the senses,
One becomes a siddha,
With eight powers and treasures.
By conquering the senses,
One becomes a warrior.
By conquering the senses,
One becomes pure.
By conquering the senses,
One becomes virtuous and great.
By conquering the senses,
One becomes pleasing to Ram.
By conquering the senses,
One gains everything.
By conquering the senses,
One becomes a sannyasi.
By conquering the senses,
One becomes an udasi.
By conquering the senses,
One fulfils all one's aims.
By conquering the senses,
One becomes worthy of all things.
By conquering the senses,

One is freed from doubt,
And nothing remains
Of the world.
By conquering the senses,
One shares bliss
And enters Hari's court.
By conquering the senses,
One becomes a conqueror.
By conquering the senses,
One becomes a friend of the spirit.
By conquering the senses,
One practices meditation
And becomes one with the Lord.
By conquering the senses,
One meets with God.
By conquering the senses,
One becomes liberated
In this very life.
Śukdev said:
Charaṇdās, listen to me—
By conquering the senses,
One becomes Guru
And Gurudeva.

VI—1 The Task of the Mind

When the senses rule the mind,
The mind becomes disorderly.
Forgetful, you frolic in the world,
Enchanted by its many hues.

Waves of anger cover you,
Remnants of your youth.
Sometimes other waves arise,
Filled with passion.

Sometimes greedy desires arise,
Coloring everything you see.
Sometimes delusions and fantasies arise,
Coloring everything with illusions.

The mind plays
All these games.
This is how the world manifests itself:
As a vain fantasy of the mind.

Now hear of the mind's wisdom.
Sometimes the mind is a householder.
Sometimes the mind is a lonely lover.
Sometimes the mind is afflicted.
Sometimes the mind is sad.
Sometimes the mind is a woman.
Sometimes the mind is a beggar.
Sometimes the mind runs around.
Sometimes the mind speaks dishonestly.
Sometimes the mind boasts of one's family.
Sometimes the mind has no ears or nose.
Sometimes the mind beats a drum.
Sometimes the mind is merciful and righteous.
Sometimes the mind is a generous donor.
Sometimes the mind refuses to give anything.
Charaṇdās says: Understand the mind.
Recognize it in all its manifestations.

Many colors, many forms,
Many opinions and many desires;
Samsara manifests itself in many ways,
Over and over again.

The mind is a pleasure-loving king.
The mind is a renounced yogi.

The mind is a devotee of Hari.
The mind is a skilful yogi.
The mind is a subtle wise man.
The mind is an ascetic, chanter and meditator.
The mind is one who speaks with compassion.
The mind is a murderer.
The mind is a Jain, a widow and a warrior.
The mind is a wise sage in Banaras.
The mind is the pilgrimage site, the vow,
And the person who fasts.
The mind is mistress and maid.
The mind is goddess and god.
No one knows the secret of the mind.
The mind is a lover,
The king and his subjects.
Charaṇdās says:
The mind is everything.

Until you know your mind
You can never become a Sādhu.
Until you abandon
Desire for the world,
You will never know
The mysterious secret.

Until you know your mind,
You will never know
The ineffable essence;
You will never be free
Of the 84 births,
You will be born
Over and over again.

VI—2 How to Conquer the Mind

Bring your mind

To the circle of saints.
Listen to stories
Of Hari's great deeds.

Instead of wanting to paint the world
In multiple hues,
Why not paint yourself
In Kṛṣṇa blue?
That is the wise thing to do.

Meditating on Hari
Will drown you
In devotion to Ram.
Apply yourself to this yoga
And resonate
With the unstruck sound.

If you free the mind from desire,
Everything else will fall away.
As other colors fade,
Brahma's lustre will deepen.
It will drive away
Karma, delusion and fear.

Śukdev told me this,
He showed me
How to change my mind.

The mind wastes your life,
Leaving wisdom's lamp
To sputter and die.
It wanders around, acting blindly,
And never allows you
To meet the Beloved.

It runs in various directions,
Seeking new experiences.
It becomes a beggar,
When it could be a king.

The five senses are fed
By sensual experiences.
Great kings can be destroyed
And become stupid fools.

Fools subsist on poisons.
In the end, they lose everything.
They do not sing bhajans.
They hold only ashes.

Their minds are unstable
And endlessly break apart.
Charaṇdās says: There is no place
They can call their home.

Wisemen and renunciants too,
Bow down their heads.
Their minds make them afraid.
They drown in midstream.

The mind is like a ghost
That runs around,
Gnashing its teeth.
It runs up and down
A bamboo pole,
Aimlessly.

When the mind is fixed in the Self,
It turns inwards.
When there is nowhere to go,

Distortions fade away.

Do not let your mind be divided,
By going around in circles.
Practise contemplation.
Understand your mind,
Through contemplation
And meditation.

Now I will tell you another way.
Listen carefully to my words.
If you chant Ram's Name in your mind,
Your fickleness will fade away.

As your mind tires, stabilize your breath,
And fix your gaze
On the tip of your nose.
If you can do this, you will find the secret
Your Guru knows.

Stop the senses, stop the mind,
This is the best way.
Charaṇdās says: This is the best way,
The best way to practice.

Use the mind to control the senses,
Use the breath to control the mind.
Use the unstruck sound to control the breath.
Withdraw yourself
Into the unstruck sound.

This is called "Samadhi."
When the mind is stabilized,
The traces of desire
From countless births

Are burned away.

Bring the senses into the mind,
The mind into the awareness,
The awareness into meditation on Hari.
Withdraw in this way.

When there are no more traces of desire,
You will never be reborn
Into this world.
Guru Śukdev said:
You will be
Liberation itself.

Chapter 16: On Telling Lies

I have told you the secret
Of how to conquer the mind.
I will speak of the difference
Between truth and lies.

Whoever tells a lie
Falls into sin.
The lie will stay with you,
Life after life,
Bringing suffering
And the threefold miseries.

It is evil to speak a lie.
You will fall from righteousness
Into disease.
A liar will swear a hundred times
That he is telling the truth.
Each lie creates new karma.

A liar will slander and be wicked.
A liar will fall in other people's eyes.
No one trusts a liar.
No one asked him to lie.

A liar will not be devoted to Hari.
A liar will fall into a pit.
A liar will be beaten by Yama,
The King of Death.
A liar will suffer
84 lakh births.

It is a great offence to lie.
Those who lie
Will never be liberated.
A liar will not find the Guru,
Will not find Ram,
Will have no rest.

Śukdev told me:
All liars go to hell.

Smear their faces
With shit;
Frighten them
And make them ashamed.
Teach them fear.

The liar is a murderer,
A cheat and a thief,
A crooked drunkard,
And a lecher.

A lie is a fever,
Look and consider this,
Men and women.
Pride is always a part of the lie.
One by one
Your secrets will be revealed.

It is the king of the five errors,
I want to warn you of this.
Lying is the source of all sins.
It will destroy the virtuous.

Śukdev told Charaṇdās:
Lying contains all the vices.

Chapter 17: The Truth

Without the truth,
The Sādhu will never find Ram.
Without the truth,
There can be no liberation.
The Sādhu will never find
The divine abode.

Let your tongue speak the truth,
Let your actions be filled with truth.
Let truth dwell in your mind,
Live in accordance with the truth.

Nothing in the stars
Can harm the man who tells the truth.
Nothing can defile
The man who tells the truth.
No curse can affect him,
Suffering is not part of his fate.

Truth is the greatest austerity,
Truth is the greatest vow.
It burns away all sins
And saves you from rebirth.

Truth cannot be twisted,
The truthful are righteous.
Charaṇdās says: They can never be defeated
In all the three worlds.

Ram dwells in the hearts

Of those who tell the truth.
They never play tricks,
They never deceive.
They embody the truth.
Through their meditation,
They save themselves
And others too.

Truth supports those
Who speak the truth.
They will not be touched
By the fires of suffering.
The honest thief stole a horse
And the Lord changed its color.
He stole other things too
And was always saved by the truth.
The powers of truth are endless.
Sādhus and Sants know them all.

A million tales tell one story,
The truthful person is creation's best jewel.
Find the truth
And you will know true bliss.
Śukdev told me this.

Truthful Sādhus and liars
Both receive honours;
The truthful are more highly regarded
And are never criticized.

Chapter 18: Complete Devotion to the Guru

Do what the Guru says,
Not what you want.
Hearing my teachings,
Keep them in mind.

Without complete devotion to the Guru,
Hearing stories of Hari—
Making vows, undertaking
Endless pilgrimages,
Will all be in vain.

Now I will tell you of the signs
Of complete devotion to the Guru.
Whoever understands these signs
And follows them closely,
Will have complete devotion to the Guru.

First. Do not lie to the Guru,
He will discover your deceitfulness.
Second. Don't just touch his feet,
Really bow before him.

Third. Honor his commands.
These are the signs
Of complete devotion.
Salute all those you meet
Who take the Guru's Name.

Those who share in the Guru's nature
Are his equal.

Śukdev told me: The Guru
And his gurubhai
Are one and the same.

Honor the Guru's associates,
Place your head at their feet.
Sip the water used to wash their feet.
Accept their teachings
As God's own word.

Hold close to your heart
The person who wears
The Guru's mantle.
Honor the Guru's throne,
Walk carefully around it.

He mercifully allowed me to see Him
And all my sins faded away.
When I reached the Guru's gate,
I was overjoyed to see His door.

I immediately bowed down,
Saw Him and gave Him my all.
Then I stood, with my hands still joined,
And sat at His command.

Whatever He said, I accepted,
And all of my faults faded away.
Charaṇdās says: Śukdev told me:
The person who is completely devoted
To the Guru,
Pleases Ram.

Chapter 19: The Greatness of Sādhus

Never criticize Sādhus,
Even by accident.
You will suffer in this world
And swing in hell.

If you criticize a Sādhu,
You will suffer
In mind and body.
If you criticize a Sādhu,
You will never be happy.
If you criticize a Sādhu,
You will always be poor.
If you criticize a Sādhu,
You will lose everything.

If you criticize a Sādhu,
You will go to hell
And be beaten by Yama.
If you criticize a Sādhu,
You are utterly sinful.
If you criticize a Sādhu,
You will drown.

Only idiots criticize Sādhus,
Only idiots pick faults
With saints and Sādhus.
If you criticize a Sādhu,
You are no better than a dog.
If you criticize a Sādhu,
You are a swine.

Sādhus are Ram's body.
Shame on those who criticize Sādhus.
Charaṇdās says: Renounce criticism,
Praise the devotees!

By praising Sādhus,
You praise Ram.
If you criticize Sādhus,
You criticize their Lord.

Chapter 20: Liberation from Delusion

I have spoken of the many ways
To develop religious devotion,
Now, through the grace of Śukdev,
I begin this chapter
On liberation from delusion.

If you take this chapter to heart,
You will be freed
From family life,
And come to Hari's feet.

Charaṇdās says:
Renunciation will arise
In your mind.
You will awaken from the world
And live in the fourth state.

Worship the Guru,
Abandon the world
And its turmoil,
Keep company with the pure,
Renounce family, caste and kin.

Your relations, wife, sons and family,
Are all death's snares.
Renounce everything for Ram,
Do not believe what anyone tells you.

They will hold onto you,
Pull you down into delusion's snares.
In life, you will suffer all sorts of pains,

In death, you will go to hell.

Your relations and family are devices
To trick your spirit.
The two most powerful forms of deception
Are wealth and sexual pleasure.

Sexual pleasure causes pain
And ties you in countless knots.
If you want to be happy,
Do not be tempted by sexual gratification.

Wealth makes you suffer in three ways,
There can be no doubting this:
Winning wealth is hard, keeping it is hard,
Losing it distresses everyone.

So when the desire for wealth arises,
Think about these issues.
This evil pair is the embodiment of misery.
See them in this way.

Whoever drowns in these two,
Will lose Ram.
Charaṇdās asks: How can such a person
Find Hari's home?

Cheating and scheming,
Making money,
All day and part of the night;
The rest of the night,
Spent in bed.

There is no end
To a wife's desires.

She longs for wealth,
In large amounts.

Making money to the day he dies,
Wherever he sits,
The serpent is there.
Whoever limits his heart
To his family,
Becomes a dog or a crow.

Thus will you wander
In 84 lakh births.
Abandon wealth and sensual desires,
And search for love that lasts.

The fool cannot give them up.
The wise renounce their bodies.
Wander like a deer,
Do not make a home anywhere.

Family life brings death
And constant suffering.
This is the way greed and pleasure
Steal your body away.

They play various games,
We all know that,
Take various forms,
And rob us in different ways.
Rañjīt says:
They plunder the world,
Day and night.

Their actions are bold,
Their motives are hidden.

In this way they bind you,
By hand and foot.

Deception places a noose
Around your neck.
Love puts chains
Around your feet.
The foolish, sensual lover
Is led away
In handcuffs.

You are thrown into ignorance,
And lie there,
Weeping and wailing.
When you try to escape,
Contempt and delusion
Will hold you back.

Five prison guards hold you down,
The five senses.
Train your body
And let wisdom flourish.

The family and the five senses
Have one common goal,
To snare human beings,
Through food and drink
To live in the world.

All of them are selfish,
No one has any real bond.
Whoever bows down to them
Will lament,
Age after age.

Mother, father, son and wife,
Pretend to have your interests
At heart:
Their love traps your body,
With no escape from the world.

Just as a hunter sets a trap,
With a generous gift,
The bird is snared by love,
And later it is killed.

So the trickster uses love,
Feigning innocence.
He offers you sweets,
Then takes everything.

The deer is summoned
By sweet sounds,
Then it is killed with a bullet.
Charaṇdās says:
This is how things are.

A fishing rod dangles in the water
With a morsel of meat
Attached as a bait.
The fish sees only a gift,
And ignores
Its own destruction.

Fool! Don't you see the reality?
Are you lost in your stupidity?
Are you so blinded by attraction
That you can't tell
How things really are?

Can't you see they want to cheat you;
Can't you tell love from fraud?
You follow them blindly,
Foolishly, understanding nothing.

Now I shall explain their tricks.
If you understand them,
You will become dispassionate.
Charaṇdās says:
Contemplate them well.

I will explain their tricks.
Each person is different.
Your father will say:
"You are my son.
I have faith in you.

"Learn these skills,
So that people respect
Our family's name.
Stay away from Sādhus,
Home
Is where you belong.

"We are men of the world,
We belong to a good caste
And a decent community.
Work hard, support your family.
Why bother with hymns
And holy tales?

"It is time for you
To take my place—
What I have done,
You must do too.

Follow my words
And you are sure to succeed.
Listen to me
And do what I say."

Charaṇdās says:
You will be miserable
As long as you live.
And when you die,
You will go to hell.

This is what your father will say,
While you live as a householder.
This is the nature of worldly things:
Wealth, fortune, wife and sons.

Your focus on family life
Will lead you astray
From Hari's way.
You will suffer
As long as you live,
And when you die,
You will be reborn
84 lakh times.

Now let me tell you
What your mother will say:
"You are mine,
I suckled you.
You should work hard,
Make a lot of money
And repay my love.

"A good son gets rich,
A bad son does not.

Adorn your wife with jewellery.
Arrange good marriages
For your sons and daughters.

"Worship your ancestors,
The gods and the goddesses.
Serve your family,
Provide for their future.
Then people will think well of you."

She teaches you to think of yourself
And makes you forget
The supreme path.
Born into the world
Again and again,
This is how
Things have always been.

Your mother makes sure
Nothing changes,
Charaṇdās says:
She will never teach you
The way to be wise.

A mother's love
Is a great burden.
She teaches you to acquire
A home, wealth,
A wife and sons.

Now hear a wife's tricks,
Which you should try to avoid.
She will overpower you
Trick you this way and that,
Flatter you with her words.

A wife will say:
"You are my protection,
My shelter.
I love you very much.
Never leave me
For anybody else."

She will tie you up
In eight different ways.
Her clothing, jewellery,
Body and make up,

She uses these things
To look very beautiful.

She flutters her eyelids shyly,
Enslaves you with her magic.
She will look at you with her dark eyes
And poison you with her body.

How can you escape from these people?
Śukdev told me how.

The person who gets caught
By these family ties,
Will struggle to be free
But never escape.

Look at your son,
Daughter and wife,
Know what you must do.

Women's superstitions
Will bind you as well:

Barbers, brahmins,
The rest of your family,
Shitala, burning ghats,
Goddesses and ghosts,
Planets and astrological conjunctions,
Will rule your destiny.
The *chauth* and *ahoi* fasts,
Good omens,
Sacred patterns
Which decorate the house . . .

Women have great power,
They can cause great suffering.
When you die
You will be reborn
84 lakh times.

Become a renunciant.
Give up your longing
For sensual pleasure.
Charaṇdās, Śukdev's servant, says:
Every family
Is a version of hell.

This is what your son will say,
In his endearing way:
"Goo goo gaa gaaa."
He charms you
But the bonds are so strong
You will never break free.

When he sits on your lap and laughs,
You will love him
More and more.
He is filled with corruption

And will bring you great suffering.

Although your love grows,
It will one day end;
Your mind and body will burn
On the funeral pyre.
Charaṇdās says:
If you want true happiness,
Be a renunciant.

We always worry about our children,
As long as there is breath
In our bodies.
Hari the Guru
Cannot enter our hearts;
This will destroy you completely.

Your body will die,
Leaving your son behind.
Your hopes will be wasted.
He may live like a pig,
His whole life through,
And go to hell
When he dies.

The family binds you,
The family traps you.
The family will throw you
Down into hell.
It is better
To separate yourself,
To leave them behind.

The body contains
A gang of thieves,

Unknown to you.
You think they are your friends,
They are not.
You cannot recognize them,
Even in your sleep.

Lust, anger, greed and delusion
Avoid them;
They are your enemies.
They puff some people up with pride,
And others with pride in their wife.

Feeding your ego, twisting words,
Telling lies,
This gang of thieves,
Lurks in your body.

Every day
They ruin everything you do.
Charaṇdās says:
This is how they attack you.

Many enemies live in your body.
How can you defeat
Even one of them?
Night and day they lay siege to you.
Is there no way of escaping them?

If you want to escape them,
You must take the path of renunciation.
Give up your family,
Be free of worldly desire.
Live at the feet of the divine.

If desire pierces your mind,

People will laugh at your pride.
Your sense of self will grow,
Delusion will enter your realm.

Ego and pride will bring their companions
And lay siege to your soul.
They will tie you up
And throw you back into your family.

Your family and friends will strengthen your bonds.
Each one will make you more blind than before.
Charaṇdās says: As soon as you enter your home,
The gang of thieves will make you stay.

Once you have abandoned family life,
You must not go back again.
That will lead to suffering in this world
And hell in the next.

II A Story

A man went into the forest
To live an ascetic life.
He endured the heat and the cold,
The wind and rain.
He ate dry leaves
And abandoned worldly ways.

Night and day he practised contemplation,
Lived at Hari's feet.
Hearing of his greatness,
A king came to see him,
Circled the saint and bowed down his head.

The king stood waiting, hands joined,

Wanting to be invited to sit down.
A long time passed.
The king thought to himself:

"This ascetic is so proud,
He does not recognize who I am."
After waiting a long time,
The king sat down of his own accord.

If you are dyed in Hari's love,
You have no need for kings.
Charaṇdās is never afraid
And needs nothing.

The ascetic said nothing.
The king stood up and rode away.
Filled with anger, he entered his palace,
And thought of a scheme
By which to revenge himself.

He would send a prostitute to test him,
To find out if the ascetic
Was true or false.
Then he would order the woman
To reveal the man's ruin.

The king ordered the courtesan
To go to his house.
First she sent her maid
To find out his secret:
What did he need?

Where does he eat?
When does he finish his prayers?
The servant did as she was asked

And told the courtesan everything.

He washes his face before dawn.
Then he bathes in the lake.
Charaṇdās said: He eats fruits and leaves
That fall from the trees.

The courtesan listened, afraid
That she might not be able
To captivate him.
Unless I can, the king will be angry,
And drive me out of town.

I need to be as sly as a crocodile,
If I am to send him down to hell.
I will use his noble inclinations
To awaken his passions.

Having decided this, the courtesan
Prepared all sorts of food,
And went to the ascetic's abode,
To tempt him away from Hari.

She sat determinedly and meditated
For as long as he did.
When he opened his eyes,
She bowed and said:

"I have come to see you
Because I have no son."
She set the food before him.
He neither spoke
Nor ate the food.

The day passed in this way.

He did not even touch the food.
Early the next morning,
She returned while he was bathing.

"Please sing a devotional song,
And grant me some comfort,"
She said. He was not moved
And ate fruit and leaves.

The courtesan said:
"I have come a long way.
You are known
For your compassion and mercy.
Do me the honor of tasting this food.
At least take a touch with your finger."

She pleaded, again and again.
He touched the food with his finger
And licked it.
Rañjīt says: One licks and licks.
This is how
The mind is misled.

Bowing, she folded her hands
And said:
"Taste it again,
King of sages,
Conqueror of the senses."

He took a whole finger full
And put it in his mouth.
She had caught him by his fingertips.
Rejoicing, she returned home.

For the next four days,

She stayed away, in bed.
It was a cunning plan.
On the fifth day, he asked:
"Where have you been?"

When she saw his affection,
She became more cunning.
She brought no food
But talked of different dishes.

"I want to serve you
By offering various dishes.
Please visit my home."
Charaṇdās says:
That was her ploy.

I have beaten him
By turning his practices
Against him.
I have won him over, slowly,
By the taste of the tongue.

She prepared different dishes
And brought them to him.
She said: "This is holy prasadam,
Please accept this humble gift.

"Because it is holy,
You must eat it all.
It is a sin not to finish this food,
And you have said
That you are a Sādhu."

As the courtesan spoke,
The ascetic thought:

I have put my hand into a serpent's hole;
The more I eat,
The more I am lost.

The courtesan told him:
"I will bring you food
Offered to the Lord.
This is a holy deed.
It will purify
Your body and mind."

Having caught him, the prostitute
Returned home and told her friends:
"I swear by the God of Love,
I'll bring him here
And show you what I've done."

Enslaved by the taste of his tongue,
Conquered by her sweet words.
Sometimes the prostitute, sometimes her maid,
Delivered him the holy dishes.

Sometimes he came out to wait.
He ate all the various dishes.
Sometimes she sent her maid,
Saying: "I am not free to come,
My lord."

She knew
That now he served her,
He no longer cared for his asceticism
Or devotional practices.

One day she came and said:
"Will you come to my house

And sanctify it by your presence?"
Her words were sweet
But he was not persuaded.

So she waited and tried a different tactic.
She worked her magic
And won his heart.
She increased her allure,
And used her eyes.

One morning she convinced him
To come to her home.
Oh Charaṇdās! Even then
He could not see the thief.

He was happy at her house
And stayed there eight days.
He was her slave
And enjoyed all five senses.

The conqueror of the senses
Went to the prostitute's house.
His ascetic powers had left him,
His feeble heart
Was shattered.
He gave up
Meditating on Ram.

See how strong your enemies are,
Inside the home.
They can bind you in chains
And keep you in a cell.
Then the prostitute went to the king
And told him
How she had cheated the ascetic.

She explained step by step
How she had tricked the monk.
The king began to laugh.
"Bring him to me," he said,
"And let me see his face."

The courtesan went home
And said to the ascetic:
"The king wants to see you.
He is the one who feeds us.

"Let us go there;
Bless him by your presence.
Then he will be merciful
And treat us kindly.
He always says
That we are his own.
The king would like us to come each day
And keep him company.

"Treat his palace as your home.
Come on, get up,
Don't be shy."
The ascetic followed the girl
To the king's courtroom.

They went and bowed down;
The king remained on his throne,
Then touched their heads.
Laughing he said: "Kindly consider
This town as your own.

I am honoured by your presence in my palace.
Blessed is she who has brought you here."

The ascetic replied: "You are already blessed,
Your majesty. You enable countless persons
To achieve great deeds.

"As soon as I saw your splendour,
I knew you had been an ascetic
In a past life.
No one gains a kingdom
Without great spiritual merit.
The Vedas and Puranas tell us that.

"I am blessed to have seen you."
The king was astonished
At the ascetic's words,
And gave great wealth
To the prostitute.

The ruler then explained
His careful, deceitful plan.
"One day I went to you,
I saw your holy presence
In the forest.

"I stood beside you for a long time.
You neither spoke
Nor opened your eyes.
Today all of that has been reversed.
You have come here
And shown me yourself
As you really are."

The ascetic immediately understood.
He renounced the woman,
Stood up, and returned to the forest.
Charaṇdās says: He became a wandering mendicant

Once more.

Those who live under the spell of the senses
Seldom change.
They try to repent,
They sigh and they suffer.

The five thieves cause great pain,
They hold the body in this world.
They inflict great pain
On body and mind,
And lead to great sin.

They trick you
And create much karma.
They take you to Yama's 56 hells,
Make you wander in 84 lakh births
And burn you in the womb.

You suffer when you are born
You suffer when you die.
They destroy the human body.
The senses shake the three worlds:
The city of the gods,
The realm of death,
And the underworld.

How did I find liberation?
When I gained control of my senses,
When I received my Master's mercy,
When my Master laid his hand on my head.

Selfishness is natural—it joins you
To your family, friends,
Relatives and community,

Only a compassionate Guru
Will tell you the supreme truth.

The supreme truth will end your suffering.
It will stop your grieving.
There is no happiness in the ego,
Don't even think about it.

The anxious person
Bears many burdens.
Your body burns,
Although there are no flames;
You roast on a funeral pyre,
While you are still alive.

The anxious body is a serpent,
It has no mouth
And knows no words.
You hear it rattle
And are lost at once.
It will eat you, again and again.

Anxiety sets the heart on fire.
Charaṇdās says:
If you fix your attention
On Hari's feet,
The flames will never take hold.

Know that the home is filled
With the poison of worldly desire.
Place no hope in the world,
Fix your mind on Hari.

The waters of desire
Flow through rivers of hope.

When the Supreme arises,
Your heart will be free.
It will never be shaken.

Without stability,
There can be no meditation,
There can be no prayer.
If you want to be devoted to Hari,
You must give up worldly desires.

As long as you are attracted to the world,
You will suffer endless pain.
The home is the doorway to anxiety
And to great fear.

The moment you leave the world,
You will find great peace,
Supreme bliss will arise.
You will not give anything,
You will not receive anything.

All that will remain
Is devotion to Hari.
Nothing will obstruct you.
When Ram makes you His own,
He takes you by the hand.

This will make you happy, friend.
Set your mind on losing your shackles.
You won't get another chance like this,
Why waste this human birth?

Wealth and home are fickle friends,
Why wait to repent?
Why regret what you have lost

And live as if there is no other way?

Every moment is priceless.
Awake! Awake!
Sleep no more!
Take control of your home.
Death is coming to meet you.

You should think: Death is coming
To take me to hell.
Śukdev said: Listen, my servant,
Charaṇdās, make your dwelling
At Hari's lotus feet.

Don't delay,
Realize this—
Charaṇdās says:
Life is a battlefield.

Life quickly passes, it is like
The shadow of a tree.
To awaken to devotion,
You must free yourself
From the embrace of the world.

You have been snared by the world,
Trapped inside it,
Like the parrot on a prepared branch.
Do not be deceived.

Like the monkey with its fist
Clenched inside a jar.
Everyone laughs.
The solution is simple:
Release your grip.

The fish catches itself
By swallowing the hook.
The goat chases the reflection of a mountain
And drowns in the lake.

The bird flies into the net
And cannot escape.
The elephant falls into the pit
Chasing the waiting female.

The deer is attracted by the lute.
Everything is easily caught
By fickle desire.
You are like this too.

You have trapped yourself,
The world didn't do it.
Charaṇdās says:
Desire destroys us all.

The way to liberation
Is to abandon desire for the world.
Know this
And live accordingly.

Why regret your mistakes?
Why repent over and over?
If you don't break your bonds,
Your life will be in vain.

Live separate from the world.
Always contemplate Hari.
Your body on the earth,
Your breath fixed

In the Supreme Lord.

Like a woman longing
For her absent lover,
So the devotees live in the world
But think only of Hari.

Like a miser,
Who buries his treasure,
His consciousness is fixed on his money,
His mind never wavers.

Shed your body
Like a snake,
Find a place
And sit in meditation.
While you have hopes,
You will have desires.
End your wandering.

Fix your thoughts on Govinda.
This is how to live in the world.
Leave your body and find Hari,
Cling to His lotus feet.

Renounce the world,
Become dispassionate.
All eight watches, sixty hours
Meditate with full awareness.

Bear no enmity,
Meditate in a humble manner.
In the end you will be liberated
And pass through the world,
Peacefully.

Charaṇdās says:
This is humility.
Who knows what might happen to others
Struck by illusion's arrows?

If you meditate on compassion,
Gentleness, humility,
Forgiveness, virtue
And tranquillity,
You will be liberated.

Hari has these qualities,
He has shown them to me.
If you become like this,
There will be love
Between Hari and yourself.

Fix your love on Hari,
Serve other people.
Dwell in the one Ram,
And everything else
Will fade away.

Don't love the temporal,
Love the eternal.
Renounce the lie,
Embrace the truth.

Hari's Name is the truth,
The world is a lie.
Śukdev told me:
Meditate on this.

Draw away from the ten senses,

Taste the fruit of eternal existence.
Contemplation is your true nature,
Set your mind on that.

Bathe in the lake of your mind.
Use your breath
As beads on a rosary.
Become the swan
That sips the nectar.
Escape karma's jaws.

This is "unchanted chanting,"
Chant but withdraw your senses,
Like a turtle within its shell,
Turn inside yourself.

See what is coming,
Know what has gone.
Maintain a balanced consciousness.
Charaṇdās, fix these things
In your heart.

Drown in the syllable "so,"
Find bliss in "ham."
Few people know that this is the way
To contemplate truth.

Swing your awareness
Up and down,
Between your solar plexus
And your nostrils.
Utter bliss will arise.
The root of pain
Will be destroyed.

Bathe your breath
In the ocean of Brahma.
Your impurities will be washed away.
And no sins will remain.

Why do you bother walking
To the 68 pilgrimage sites?
Charaṇdās says: Turn around
And come home.

Control your breath.
Make it your dwelling.
On the out-breath say "Hari."
On the in-breath say "Shyam."

Those who breathe
Without taking the Name,
Waste their lives.
Chant "Ram"
With every breath you take.
This is the foundation
Of true meditation.

Up and down,
Chant only "Ram."
The crooked will become straight.
You'll never lose the fruits
Of this practice.
That is impossible.

Take the Name
While you eat and drink,
Sit, walk and sleep.
The Name is sacred
And illuminates everything.

It raises the fallen,
Makes men into gods.
It turns the gods into Hari.
It removes all duality.

We wandered until the day
We took a human birth.
When will such a chance come again?
Take the Name at once.

Whether you are at home or abroad,
If you think of the Name
There will be no difference
Between your home and the temple.

If you perform austerities,
Yoga, sacrifices and acts of charity,
Without taking the Name,
Charaṇdās says:
You have wasted your time.

The Name is the highest,
The source of all creation.
Churn the eighteen Puranas and four Vedas,
Use their essence
To make your mantra.

This has been seen in every era:
Those who chant the Name
Attain great fame.
They move forwards
And never go back.

Your liberation is as sure

As that of the sages
Who first sang
The Vedas and Puranas,
This is certain.

Abandon suffering's rod,
Renounce anger and illusion.
Śukdev told me: Devote yourself
To praising Ram.

Make a rosary of Hari's virtues,
Keep it on your tongue.
Contemplate His actions,
Praise Him always.

Watch Him. Watch Him.
Sing of His glory.
Keep His excellencies
Before your mind.

There is no painter like Him,
No printer like Him,
No craftsman like Him,
In all the world.

He did many marvellous things,
Beyond compare.
Contemplate His acts,
On land and water,
Sky and air.

He was a Gardener
And grew the world,
With every kind of flower.
You may lose your mind

Watching it blossom.

Sometimes the world appears,
Sometimes it fades.
You can play endless games
And be lost in each one of them.

The director invented these games
And every possible move.
He created these various distractions
To show you His skill.

You rejoice at the sight
And praise its attributes.
Charaṇdās says: the wise man
Knows the creator.

Your love grows
But you don't know why.
You forgot the secret
And never cultivated virtue.

You forgot Ram from the beginning
And focused on wealth and pleasure instead.
This is why you wander from one life to the next
And are born again and again.

"What has gone will never return
So cling to this now"—
What foolishness!
Repeat Hari's Name,
Be free from passion.
This is the Guru's teaching.

Don't waste your life sleeping,

Your time is short.
Awaken, Charaṇdās!
Don't be lazy.

You lose a lot,
While you are asleep.
You gain a lot,
While you are awake:
Your consciousness glows,
Your face shines.

Contemplate Hari by day,
Keep watch and meditate
At night.
Eat when you are hungry,
Stay awake while you can.

If you cannot stay awake
All four watches,
Then keep your vigil
For half the night,
Meditate and chant,
Sing songs of praise.

If you can't do that,
Then pass two watches in faith
And wake before dawn,
Sit and stand, repeat the Name,
And lovingly contemplate the Lord.

If you can't be awake for the last watch,
You should cover your head in shame.
If you don't remember the Creator,
Your existence will have no meaning.

If you can't be awake for the last watch,
Then you will never know
Who you are.
You will go to hell,
After a painful death.

If you can't be awake for the last watch,
And don't repeat your Guru's teachings,
If you continue to sleep
With your mouth wide open,
Sin will enter in.

If you are awake for the last watch,
And sing songs of praise,
Charaṇdās says: Your soul
Will surely be liberated.

If you are awake for the last watch,
Drinking spiritual nectar,
Sensuality's bonds will be broken
And your soul will be immortal.

Birth will not touch you,
Death will not touch you,
Reincarnation will not touch you,
If you are awake
For just one watch,
Sit and sing of the Lord.

Everyone is awake
During the first watch,
The second is lost
In sensuality,
The third is stolen,
The fourth is for the yogi.

The code of conduct
For the supreme renunciant
Is to be awake all eight watches,
All sixty hours,
Contemplating Hari.

How can Ram's lovers sleep,
Separated from Him?
They are afflicted by love's arrows,
Pierced to the heart.

Renouncing the world
Is easy for them.
Love means nothing;
Neither do personal rights.
They are no longer householders;
They wear the renunciant's robes.

Their hearts are fixed in renunciation.
They meditate on Him,
Wherever they are.
At home or away.
They burn
And lose all duality.

The sleeping focus on the world.
The awakened turn to Ram.
They are aware of the spirit
Which has no dawn,
Has no dusk.

Always eager to meet Ram,
They never sleep.
How can they rest in their beds,

How can they live,
Without their friend,
Without Hari?

Who can meet Hari?
A fortunate few.
How can they abandon Hari
And remain in the world?

Few know the difference
Between sleep and wakefulness.
The group of Sādhus is awake,
While it is night for everyone else.

Those who stay awake
Devoted to Hari,
Pass over to the other shore.
Those who stay awake
Devoted to the world,
Drown in the ocean of existence.

Will smoking a pipe
Make you more awake?
Will sensual embraces
Make you more awake?
Will serving the world
Make you more awake?
Or earning money
And keeping up with the world?

Such a birth is wasted
In foolishness and ignorance.
The longings of your heart
Will lead to 84 lakh births.

Come, take refuge with the True Guru,
Accept every word he says.
Those who deny him will suffer much
And never find happiness.

If you don't fall at the True Guru's feet,
You have not really searched for Hari.
You are an ass, a dog or a pig,
A deer lost in the forest.

If you fill your belly and sleep,
You live like an animal.
If you covet other men's women,
You are a fool.

The man who eats everything he finds,
Who sleeps when his belly is full,
Lays down and sleeps until dawn,
Has the body of a pig.

The man who speaks,
Without speaking of Hari,
Is the ghost of a dog.
Rañjīt says:
He is a field
Offering nothing to eat
But dust.

The man who bears many burdens
On his back,
Who does not chant Hari's Name,
Is an ass.

The man who eats everything
Can never think clearly.

How can Hari's Name
Purify his mind?

Eat plain food,
Sleep less.
Without devotion,
Your body
Is wasted.

Life quickly passes,
Like light in a well,
Like the shadow of a running deer.
It never stops,
Not even for a moment.

Understand this now.
Learn devotion,
Don't waste a moment.
Give yourself to Hari,
This is the only way.

Don't believe the world,
Fix your mind on the True Guru.
Keep the Guru in your heart
And you will be quickly purified.

The True Guru is more than a teacher,
The True Guru is the embodiment
Of Parameswar.
The shade of liberation
Will protect you
From the glare of the world.

First, speak of the True Guru
As your benefactor.

Second, know the True Guru
To be your mother.
Third, recognize the True Guru
As the one who feeds you.
Fourth, know the True Guru
To be your father.
Fifth, the True Guru
Is your teacher.
Sixth, the True Guru
Whispers the mantra
Into your ear.
Seventh, the True Guru
Helps you renounce the world,
Gives you the gift
Of liberation's domain.
So says Charaṇdās.

When you meet the Guru
Say: "I give you
All that I have."
When you meet the True Guru
You will say:
"I am blessed
To have received the Name."

The True Guru whispers the mantra
Into your ear,
And brings you to Ram.
The True Guru
Shows you
Liberation's domain.

Many false teachers
Wander the streets,
Making disciples

In each and every home.
All they care about
Is your money.

The True Guru
Beats the drum of war
And summons you
To worship Ram.
All you have to do is
Give him your head.

Śukdev is a True Guru.
Understand this,
Keep it in your heart.
Take refuge in Śukdev,
Says Charaṇdās.

This teaching is worth more
Than every sacrifice;
But I freely give it to you.
Once I was selfish
And swayed by my heart,

I asked the True Guru
And He gave me poverty.
He took away my pride
And made me humble.

Father, Supreme Guru,
Hear me, Śukdev, True Master,
My one request:
Make me a Sādhu.

You are the Abode of Bliss
For devotees of every era.

Let me serve Your feet
And always bow before You.

Your strength is unlimited,
Your divine drama unending.
Charaṇdās says:
You are Bhagwan.

As Narayan,
You created the physical world
To be an embodiment of Yourself.
Then Lakshmi appeared
With water
And bright colors.

Brahma arose
From the lotus in Your navel.
Shiva appeared
At Brahma's brow.

The four Vedas and Vishnu
The whole world
Appeared in an instant;
The formless
Assumed form.
Charaṇdās says:
This is how the mind works.

It is unmovable Ram
Who lives in the Beyond.
It is unmovable Ram
Who came to Mathura.

It is unmovable Ram
Whom the yogis contemplate.

It is unmovable Ram
Whom Sita took as her husband.

It is unmovable Ram
Who dwells in all places and times.
It is unmovable Ram
Who supports the Sants.

It is unmovable Ram
Whom Charaṇdās follows.
It is unmovable Ram
Whom you will find
Inside your own body.

Maya is a deceptive snare,
Fix your eyes
On the company of Sādhus.
Whoever dons Ram's robes
Turns his body to gold.

Understand the nature of the mind,
And your insight will be complete.
Why bother with endless noise
When the unstruck sound is ringing?

Go inside your own body,
Ascend and descend,
Rise above the four lower chakras,
Use the breath
To climb Mount Meru.

Make your home
In the midst of heaven,
Where there is neither heat nor cold.
Meditate on the state

Which is free from fear.

Duryodhana and Ravana have gone,
And all the Yadav clan.
Charaṇdās says: Nothing remains,
Everything passes.

You were born at dawn.
It is noon:
Why delay?
Consider this carefully:
Night is coming quickly.

The whirlpool of worry
Has fixed its eye on you.
Each moment, each instant,
Your life is under attack.

Wife, son, wealth, everything
Will not bring lasting happiness.
You will realize this
When all fall away.

Charaṇdās says:
Why don't you abandon
Sensuality and desire
Right now?
Your life glides past
Like a boat on a river.

Youthful ambitions and duty
Are meaningless actions.
Oh, the suffering of 84 lakh births!
Fool, why don't you renounce the world?

Sit in the company of Sādhus,
Cross over on dharma's ferryboat.
Be firm in the Guru's wisdom,
Practise loving devotion.

How can you be free
When the family binds you in suffering?
You will be born in hell,
Over and over again.
Why don't you change your ways?

Charaṇdās says:
Why don't you abandon
Sensuality and greed?
Why don't you
Adore Ram
And sing His praises?

Misled in the world,
Overshadowed by death,
Your affection grows
For your wife, daughter and son.
They share your home,
But when you die,
You die on your own.

The pains of death
Will take everything from you.
Search for the Beloved, says Ram.
Charaṇdās says:
Awaken, foolish man.
Nothing has any meaning
Without Ram.

You cover your body with sacred ash.

What do you have inside?
At the hour of your suffering
You will have
Neither companion nor kin.

You may be touched by the goddess Chandi,
By ghosts and Shitala's fevers.
Why don't you sing Ram's Name
And destroy the bonds of death?

Bhairav and Varahi are frauds,
False gods.
Everything happens as Hari ordains.
Can't you see this?

Charaṇdās says:
It is so cruel.
The servants of the Sants say:
"The world is blind.
It is caught
In karma's chains."

Amulets, spells, physical contortions
And countless lies
Are deceitful tricks, says Charaṇdās,
They will rob you
Of everything you own.

If you worship ghosts,
You will be born a ghost.
If you worship magic,
Your mother will be a Chamar.

If you worship the gods,
You will live in heaven.

If you worship potions,
You will meet the king of medicine makers.

If you worship alchemy,
You will have endless misfortune
And lose all your money.
This may not please you,
But I tell you the truth.

Charaṇdās says:
Why don't you believe me?
Why can't you see?
Why are you so proud
When you hear Kṛṣṇa's Name?

Mercury cannot stop you dying,
Sulphur cannot oil your body.
Many have died trying these remedies,
And been laid low in the ground.

Laid low in the ground,
They wander in vain,
Wasting their births.
They spoke of herbs and healing;
It made no difference.

Why don't you praise Hari, you fool?
Why do you waste your life?
Guru Śukdev told me:
Alchemy is bogus.

Some worship the five and seven.
Others worship the one.
Intoxicated, true Sādhus serve Ram,
With shaven heads and orange robes.

You cannot see them
Among the crowds of holy men.
Charaṇdās teaches: Understand this,
Know and accept it.

Ascetics who do not sing songs of praise,
But contemplate trivial things
Are foul fiends, says Charaṇdās,
They will wander
And fall into hell.

Those who teach others
And sing songs of praise,
Are true Sādhus, says Charaṇdās,
They will enter
Hari's kingdom.

I am a citizen
Of the realm of emptiness.
My family deity is the unstruck sound.
My lineage is the unchanted chant.
Charaṇdās says:
This is my secret.

All things come to fruition
From this *Treasury of Devotion,*
Whoever reads it, hears it, or honors it
Will attain nirvana.

I have sung this *Treasury of Devotion*
And revealed certain secrets.
Whoever understands these things with love
Will be freed from death's snare.
If you contemplate it regularly,

Says Guru Śukdev,
You will pass over
The ocean of existence.

Glory! Glory be to Lord Śukdev!
I worship You.
You have spoken
These words of blessing,
And brought my task to an end.

You have comforted me,
Removed my troubles.
You made my coward's heart brave,
I have sung these songs.

I offer sandalwood and flowers,
I bow before You.
I have sung these songs
For all who will listen,
All men and women.

Whoever recites these words,
Hears and remembers them,
With love,
Charaṇdās says,
Will become a true Sādhu.

The Hindi Text

१ गुरुमहिमा

दोहा

प्रणवों श्री मुनि व्यासजी, मम हिरदय में आय ।
भक्ति पदारथ कहत हूं, तुमहीं करो सहाय ।।१।।
प्रेम पगावन ज्ञान दे, योग जितावन हार ।
चरणदास की वीनती, सुनियो बारम्बार ।।२।।
तुम दाता हम माँगता, श्रीशुकदेव दयाल ।
भक्ति दई व्याधा गई, मेटे जगजंजाल ।।३।।
किसी काम के थे नहीं, कोउ न कौडी देह ।
गुरु शुकदेव कृपा करी, भई अमोलक देह ।।४।।
को है कोइ न जानता, गिनती में नहिं नावँ ।
गुरु शुकदेव कृपा करी, पूजन लागे पावँ ।।५।।
सीधी पलक न देखते, छूटे नाहीं छाहिं ।
गुरु शुकदेव कृपा करी, चरणोदक ले जाहिं ।।६।।
दूसर के बालक हुते, भक्ति बिना कंगाल ।
गुरु शुकदेव दया करी, हरि धन किये निहाल ।।७।।
जा धन कूं ठग ना लगै, धारि सकै नहिं लूट ।
चोर चुराय सकै नहीं, गाँठ गिरै नहिं खूट ।।८।।
बलिहारी गुरु आपने, तन मन सदके आँव ।
जीव ब्रह्म क्षणमें कियो, पाई भूली बाँव ।।९।।
हरि सेवा सोलह बरस, गुरु सेवा पल चार ।
तौ भी नहीं बराबरी, वेदन कियो विचार ।।१०।।
गुरि की सेवा साधू जानै । गुरु सेवा कह मूढ पिछानै ।।
गुरु सेवा सबहुन पर भारी । समझ करो सोई नर नारी ।।

गुरु सेवा सों विघन विनाशै। दुरमति भाजै पातक नाशै ।।
गुरु सेवा चौरासी छूटै। आवागमन का डोरा टूटै ।।
गुरु सेवा यम दण्द न लागै। ममता मरै भक्तमें जागै ।।
गुरु सेवा सूं प्रेम प्रकाशै। उनमत होय मिटै जग आशै ।।
गुरु सेवा परमातम दरशै। त्रैगुण तजि चौथापन परशै ।।
श्रीशुकदेव बतायो भेवा। चरणदास कर गुरु की सेवा ।।११।।

दोहा
गुरु सेवा जानैं नहीं, पाँय न पूजै धाय ।।
योग दान जप तप कियो, सभी अफल ह्वै जाय ।।११।।
योग दान जब तीरथ न्हाना। गुरुसेवा बिन निष्फल जाना ।।
गुरुसेवा बिन बहु पछितैहौ। फिरि फिरि यम के द्वारे जैहौ ।।
गुरुसेवा बिन अति दुख पैहौ। जगमें पशु दरिद्री ह्वै हौ ।।
गुरुसेवा बिन कौन उतारै। भवसागर सूं बाहर डारै ।।
गुरुसेवा बिन जड कह करिहै। काकी नाव बैठकी तरि है ।।
गुरुसेवा बिन कछु नहिं सरिहै। महा अंधकूपन में परि है ।।
गुरुसेवा बिन घट अँधियारा। कैसे प्रगट ज्ञान उजियारा ।।
नरक निवारण गुरु शुकदेवा। चरणदास करि तिनकी सेवा ।।

दोहा
इन्द्री जित निरवैरता, निरमोही निरद्वन्द्व ।।
ऐसो गुरुकी शरण कूं, मिटै सकल दुखद्वन्द्व ।।१२।।
राग द्वेष दोनों से न्यारे। ऐसे गुरु शिष्य कूं तारै ।।
आशा तृष्णा कुबुधि जलाई। तन मन वचन सबन सुखदाई ।।
निरालम्ब निर्भरम उदासी। निर्विकार जानौ निरवासी ।।
निर्मोहित निर्बन्द निशंका। सावधान निर्वाण अशंका ।।
सारग्रही और सरवंगी। संतोषी ज्ञानी सतसंगी ।।
अयाचीक जत निर अभिमानी। पक्ष रहित स्थिर शुंध वानी ।।
निहतरंग नाहीं परपंचा। निहकरम निरलिप्त जो संचा ।।
शीतल तासु मति है देवा। चरणदास कियो सो गुरुदेवा ।।

दोहा

सतवादी अरु शीलवंत, सुत्दृदै अरु यौगीश ।।
निश्चल ध्यान समाधि में, सो गुरु विस्वेबीश ।।१४।।
भरम निवारण भय हरण, दूर करण सन्देह ।
मुठिया खोलै ज्ञानकी, सो सदगुरु करलेह।।१५।।
सदगुरु के लक्षण कहै, ताकूं ले पहिचान ।
निरख परख कर दीजिये, तन मन धन अरु प्राण।।१६।।
ऐसा सदगुरु कीजिये, जीवित डारै मारि ।
जनम जनम की वासना, ताकूं देवै जारि ।।१६।।
सदगुरु ढिग जाइकै, सन्मुख खावै चोट ।
चकमक लग पथरी झरै, सकल जरावै खोट ।।१७।।
सदगुरु मेरा शूरमा, करै शब्द की चोट ।
मारै गोला प्रेम का, ढहै भरम का कोट ।।१८।।
मुखसेती बोलन धका, सुने न थका जु कान ।
पावनसूं थिरवा थका, सदगुरु मारा बान ।।१९।।
मैं मिरगा गुरु पारधी, शब्द लगायो बाण ।
चरणदास घायल गिरे, तनमन बींधै प्राण ।।२०।।
शब्द बाण मोहिं मारिया, लगी कलेजे माहिं ।
मार हँस शुकदेवजी, वाकी छाडी नाहिं ।।२१।।
सदगुरु शब्दी तेग है, लाग दो करता देहि ।
पीठि फेरि कायर भजै, शूरा सन्मुख लेहि ।।२२।।
सदगुरु शब्दी सेलर है, सहै धमूका साध ।
कायर ऊपर जो चलै, तौ जावै बरबाद ।।२३।।
सदगुरु शब्दी तीर है, तन मन कीयो छेद ।
बेदरदी समुझै नहीं, विरही पावै भेद ।।२४।।
सदगुरु शब्दी लागिया, नावककासा तीर ।
कसरत है निकसत नहीं, होत प्रेमकी पीर ।।२५।।
सदगुरु शब्दी बाण है, अँग अँग डारै तोड ।
प्रेम खेत घायल गिरे, टाँका लगै न जोड ।।२६।।
सदगुरु शब्दे मोरिया, पूरा आया वार ।
प्रेमी झूझे खेत में, लगा न राखा तार ।।२७।।
ऐसी मारी खैंचकर, लगी वार गइ पार ।

जिनका आपा ना रहा, भये ,रूप ततसार ।।२८।।
सदगुरु के मारे मुये, बहुरि न उपजै आय ।
चौरासी बन्धन छूटै, हरिपद पहुँचे जाय ।।२९।।
सदगुरु के वचनौं मुये, धन्य जिन्होंके भाग ।
त्रैगुण ते ऊपर गये, जहाँ दोष नहिं राग ।।३०।।
वचन लगा गुरुदेव का, छूटै राज के साज ।
हीरा मोती नारि सुत, गज घोडा अरु बाज ।।३१।।
वचन लगा गुरु ज्ञान का, रूखे लागे भोग ।
इन्द्रकि पदवी लौ उन्हें, चरणदास सब रोग ।।३२।।
सद्‌गुरु ढूँढा पाइये, नहीं सुहेला होय ।
शिष्य भी पूरा कोइ है, सानी माटी जोय ।।३३।।
जाति वरण कुल आश्रम, मान बडाई खोय ।
जब सद्‌गुरु के पग लगै, साँच शिष्य है सोय ।।३४।।
गुरु के आगै राखै माथा । कहै पाप दुख मेटौ नाथा ।।
मैं आधीन तुम्हारो दासा । देहु आपने चरणन वासा ।।
यह तन मन ले भेंट चरायो । अपनी इच्छा कुछ न रहायो ।।
जो चाहै सो तुमहीं करो । या भाँडे में जो कुछ भरो ।।
भावै धूप छाँह में डारो । भावै बोरो भावै तारो ।।
गुण पौरुष कुछ बुधि नहिं मेरी । सब विधि शरण गही प्रभु तेरी ।।
मैं चुकई अरु तुम किय डोरा । मैं जो फिरूं सब तुम्हरे जोरा ।।
मैं अब बैठा नाव तुम्हारी । आशा नदी सुं करिये पारी ।।
भ्रमर जाल जग सूं मोहिं काढो । हाथ जोरि चरणदासा ठाढो ।।

दोहा
गुरु के आगे जाय करि, ऐसे बोलै बोल ।
कछू कपट राखै नहीं, अर्ज करै मन खोल ।।३५।।
यह आपा तुम कूं दिया, जित चाहौ तित राख ।
चरणदास द्वारे परो, भावै झिडको लाख।।३६।।
ऋद्धि सिद्धि फल कछू न चाऊं । जगत कामना को नहिं लाऊं ।।
और कामना मैं नहिं राखूं । रसना नाम तुम्हारो भाखूं ।।
राज भोग का मोहिं न साँसा । नहीं इन्द्र पदवी लौ आसा ।।
चौरासी में बहु दुख पायों । ताते शरण तिहारी आयों ।।

मुक्त होने की मन में आवै । आवागमन सों जीव डरावै ।।
राम भक्ति की चाह हमारे । याते पकडे चरण तुम्हारे ।।
प्रेम प्रीति में हिरदा भीजै । यही दान दाता मोहिं दीजै ।।
अपना कीजै गहिये बाहीं । धरिये शिरपर हाथ गोसाई ।।
चरणदास को लेहु उबारे । मैं अण्दा तुम सेवनवारे ।।

दोहा

अण्दा ज्यों आगे गिरै, जब गुरु लेवे सेइ ।
करै बरामबर आपनी, शिष्यहि को निस्सन्देह ।।३७।।
अपना करि सेवन करै, तीन भांति गुरुदेव ।
पंजा पक्षी कुंजवन, कछुवा दृष्टि जु भेव ।।३८।।
जो वै बिछुरैं घडी भी, तो गंदा होय जाय ।
चरणदास यों कहत है, गुरु को राखु रिझाय ।।३९।।
पितु सों माता सौगुणा, सुतको राखै प्यार ।
मनसेती सेवन करै, तन सों डाट रु गार ।।४०।।
जो देवैं दुरशीश भी, होहो लगै अशीश ।
सेवन करि समरथ कियो, उनपर वारौं शीश ।।४१।।
माता सों हरि सौगुणा, जिनसै सौ गुरुदेव ।
प्यारे कैं औगुणा हरैं, चरणदास शुकदेव ।।४२।।
काचे भांडे सों रहै, ज्यों कुम्हार को नेह ।
भीतर सों रक्षा करै, बाहर चोटैं देह ।।४३।।
दृष्टि पडे गुरुदेवकी, देखत करै निहाल ।
और गति पलटैं तबै, कागा होत मराल ।।४४।।
दया होय गुरुदेवकी, भजै मान अरु मैन ।
भोग वासना सब छुटै, पावै अतिही चैन ।।४४।।
जब सदगुरु किरपा करैं, खोलि दिखावै नैन ।
जग झूठा दीखन लगै, देह परेकी सैन ।।४६।।

अष्टपदी

गुरु बिन और न जान मान मेरो कहो । चरणदास उपदेश विचारतही रहो ।
वेदरूप गुरु होय के कथा सुनवाई । पंडित को धरि रूप कि अरथ बतावई ।।
गुरु ह्वै शेष महेश तोहिं चेतन करै । गुरु ब्रह्मा गुरु विष्णु होय खाली भरै ।।

कल्प वृक्ष गुरुदेव मनोरथ सब सरै । कामधेनु गुरुदेव क्षुधा तृष्णा हरै ।।
गंगा सम गुरु होय पाप सब धोवई । शशधर सम गुरु होय तपत सब खोवई ।।
सूरज सम गुरु होय तिमिर सब लेवई । पार ब्रह्म गुरु होय मुक्तिपद देवई ।।
गुरुही को ध्यान नाम गुरुको जपौ । आपा दीजै भैंट पूजन गुरुही थपौ ।।
समरथ श्रीशुकदेव कहा महिमा करौं । अस्तुति कही न जाय शीश चरणन धरौं ।।

दोहा
हरि रूठे कुछ डर नहीं, तू भी दे छिटकाय ।
गुरु को राखौ शीश पर, सब विधि करैं सहाय ।।४७।।

अष्टपदी
गुरु को तजि हरि सेवा कभी नहिं कीजिये ।
बेमुख को नहिं ठौर नरक में दीजिये।।
गुरु निंदक नहिं मुक्त गर्भ फिर आवई ।
चौरासी लाख भुक्ति महादुख पावई ।।
प्रथम करै गुरु देखि परखि चरणौं परै ।
उनकी घारन ध्यान टेक उर में धरै ।।
गुरु को रामहिं जान कृष्ण सम जानिये ।
गुरु नृसिंह अवतार जु वामन मानिये ।।
गुरु को पूरण जान जु ईश्वर रूपही ।
सब कुछ गुरु को जान जु यह बात अनूपही।।
हरि गुरु एकहि जान यह निश्चय लाइये ।
दुबिधाही को बोझ जु वेग बगाइये ।।
धर्म पिता गुरु जान जु दृढता राखिये ।
लाज सकुचि करि कान ढीठता नाखिया ।।
मेरा यह उपदेश हिये में धारियो ।
गुरु चरणन मन राखि सेव तन गारियो ।।
जो गुरु झिरकै लाख तौ मुख मोडियो ।
गुरु सों नेह लगाय सबन सों तोडियो ।।
जो शिष्य सांचा होय तो आपा दीजियो ।
चरणदास की सीख समझकर लीजियो।।
मोको श्रीशुकदेव यही समझाइयो ।

वेद पुराणन माहिं जु योंहीं गाइयो ॥

दोहा

गुरु अस्तुति कह कहि सकै, चरणदास कह बुद्धि ।
भक्तों की अब कहत हौं, जो वै देवैं शुद्धि ॥४८॥

२ भक्तमहिमा

दोहा

भक्तन की अस्तुति किये, तन मन हियो सिराय।
कलि का मैल रहै नहीं, बुधि उज्ज्वल ह्वै जाय ।।४९ ।।
साधन की सेवा करौ, चरणदास चित लाय।
जनम मरण बंधन कटै, जगत व्याधि छुटि जाय ।।५०।।
जो भक्तों की सेवा करै। यम के फन्दे नाहीं परै।
जिन साधों का दर्शन देखा। तिनका यम सों रहा न लेखा ।।
जो भक्तों को शीश नवावै। तन छूटै जब नहिं दुख पावै ।।
जो कोइ साधु संग में रलै। जठर अग्नि में नाहीं जलै ।।
जो साधों की अस्तुति भाखै। भावै भक्ति प्रेम रस चाखै ।।
जो भक्तों सों प्रीति लगावै। वह निश्चय हरि को अपनावै ।।
जो भक्तों की वाणी गावै। समझै अर्थ परमपद पावै ।।
साधु संग बिन गति नहिं होनी। क्या तपसी अरु क्या भयो मौनी ।।
चरणदास भक्तों की शरना। ह्वांई जीवन ह्वांई मरना ।।

३ भक्तलक्षण

दोहा

भक्तिभाव निर्मल दिशा, संतोषी निर्वास ।
मन राख नवधा विषे, और न दूजी आस ।।५१।।
दयावान दाता गुण पूरे । पैज धारणा वचनौ शूरे ।।
मुक्ति कामना फल नहिं चाहैं । ऋद्धि सिद्धि अरु त्यागैं लाहैं ।।
हानि लाभ जिनके नहिं टोटा । वैरी मित्र खरा नहिं खोटा ।।
मान उपमान कछू नहिं तिनकै । दुख सुख एक बराबर जिनके ।।
शुभ अरु अशुभ कछू नहिं जानै । राव रंक को ना पहिंचानैं ।।
कंचन काच बराबर देखै । जग व्योहार कछू नहिं लेखै ।।
हार जीत नहिं वाद विवाद । सदा पवित्र समझ अगाधा ।।
हर्ष शोक जिनके नहिं कबहीं । लख चौरासी प्यारे सबहीं ।।
हिंसा अकस भाव नहिं दूजा । सब जीवन की राखै पूजा ।।
चरणदास शुकदेव बतावै । ऐसै लक्षण साधु कहावै ।।

दोहा

भक्तन की पदवी बडी, इन्द्रहु से अधिकाय ।
तीन लोक के सुख तजे, लीन्हो हरि अपनाय ।।५२।।
अनन्य भक्त निष्काम जो, करै सोय चरणदास ।
चार मुक्ति वैकुण्ठ लों, सबसे रहै निरास ।।५३।।

४ साधु माहात्मय

दोहा

प्रभु अपने मुख से कह्यो, साधू मेरी देह ।
उनके चरणन की मुझे, प्यारी लागै खेह ।।५४।।
आठ सिद्धि वै ले नहीं, कनक कामिनी नाहिं ।
मेरे सँग लागे रहैं, कभी न छोडै बाहिं ।।५५।।
सब तजिकर मोकों भजै, मोहिं सेती प्रीति ।
मैं भी उनके कर बिक्यो, यही जु मेरी रीति ।।५६।।
साधु हमारी आतमा, सब से प्यारे मोहिं ।
नारद निश्चय कीजिये, साँच कहत हौं तोहिं ।।५७।।
जिनके कारण मैं रचौं, अद्भुत यह संसार ।
उनहीं की इच्छा धरूं, हर युग में अवतार ।।५८।।
प्रेमी का ऋणियां रहौं, यही हमारो सूल ।
चारि मुक्त दइ व्याज में, दै न सकौं अब मूल ।।५९।।
सर्वस दीन्हों भक्त को, देख हमारो नेह ।
निर्गुण सों सगुन भयो, धरी पशु की देह ।।६०।।
मेरे जन मो में रहें, मैं भक्तन के माहिं ।
मेरे अरु मम सन्त के, कछु भी अन्तर नाहिं ।।६१।।
साधु सोवै तहँ सोय रहूँ, भोजन सँगही जेवुँ ।
जो वह गावै प्रेम सों, मैं ताली देवूँ ।।६२।।
मम भक्ता जित जित फिरै, गवनै लागा जाँव ।
जहां तहां रक्षा करौ, भक्तवत्सल मो नाँव ।।६३।।
भक्त हमारो पग धरै, जहां धरूं मैं हाथ ।
लारे लागोही फिरौं, कबहुँ न छोड़ूं साथ ।।६४।।
मोको वश कियो जो चहै, भक्तन की करै सेव ।
उनमें ह्वैकर मैं मिलौं, करौं बहुत ही हेव ।।६५।।
पृथ्वी पावन होत है, सबही तीरथ आदि ।

चरणदास हरि यों कहैं, चरण धरैं जब साधि ।।६६।।
जिनकी महिमा प्रभु करै, अपने मुख सों भाखि ।
तिनकी कौन बराबरी वेद भरत है साखि ।।६७।।
जिनकी आशा करत हैं, स्वर्ग माहिं सब देव ।
कबहूं दर्शन पाय हैं, चरण कमलं की सेव ।।६८।।
अपने अपने लोक में, सभी करैं उत्साह ।
साधू काया छोड करि गवन करै किस राह ।।६९।।
धनि नगरी धनि देश है, धनि पुर पट्टन गाँव ।
जहँ साधूजन उपजियो ताके बलि बलि जाँव ।।७०।।
भगत जु आनैं जगत में, परमारथ के हेत ।
आप तरैं तारैं परा, मँडैं भजन के खेत ।।७१।।
भवसागर सों तारि करि, लै जावैं बहु जीव ।
साधू केवट राम के, पार मिलावै पीव ।।७२।।
काम क्रोध मद लोभ हनि, गर्व तजै जो साध ।
राम नाम हिरदै धरै, रोम रो औराध ।।७३।।
साधू महिमा को कहै, शोभा अधिक अपार ।
रसना दोय हजार सों, शेषहु जावै हार ।।७४।।
अनन्य भक्ति करि प्रेम सों, जीति लिये गोविन्द ।
चरणदास हो वश किये, पूरण परमानन्द ।।७५।।

५ सत्संगति महिमा

दोहा

तपके वर्ष हजार हूं, सत्संगति घडि एक ।
तौ भी सरबर ना करै, शुकदेव किया विवेक ।।७६।।
सत्संगति महिमा बड भाई । स्मृति वेद पुराणन गाई ।।
मुनि वसिष्ठ कहो याही भेवा । साधु संग को तरसैं देवा ।।
साधु संग को नारद जानै । सो वह पिछलौ जन्म पिछानै ।।
देखो संगति की अधिकाई । वालमीकि अरु शबरी गाई ।।
अजामील सतसंगति परिया । अनगिन पाप किये सब जरिया ।।
सत्संगति बहु पतित उधारै । अधम सरीखे मुक्ति पधारै ।।
जाट जुलाहा अरु रैदासा । संगति साधु हुआ परकासा ।।
साधुन की संगति मुकताई । चरणदास शुकदेव बताई ।।

दोहा

जब जब दर्शन राम दें, तब माँगौं सत्संग ।
चाहौं पदवी भक्ति की, चढै सु नवधा रंग ।।७७।।
कूवा सैना सदना नाई । बहुतक नीच भये उँच पाई ।।
जैसे ठार ठौर को पानी । सुरसरि मिलि भो गंगा रानी ।।
तैसे काठ लोह को तारै । ऐसे सेगति मिलि भय पारै ।।
जैसे पारस लोहा लागा । सो वह कंचन भयो सुभागा ।।
देवल तीरथ बहु मग धावै । साधुसंग बिन गति नहिं पावै ।।
ढाका पात पानके साथा । संगति मिलि गयो भूपन हाथा ।।
त्यों गोविन्द सँग गाई कुबरी । सूवा के सँग गणिका उबरी ।।
हरि भगवान में दीजै वासा । जन्म जन्म माँगै चरणदासा ।।

दोहा

ऊंची पदवी साधु की, महिमा कही न जाय ।

सुर नर मुनि जग भूपही, देखत रहे लजाय ।।७९।।

राग सारंग

करो नरहरी भक्तन को संग । दुख बिसरै सुख होय घनेरौ तन मन पसटै अंग ।।

ह्वै निष्काम मिलौ सन्तन सों नाम पदारथ मंग । जिहि पाये सब पातक नाशैं उपजै ज्ञान तरंग ।।

जो वे दया करै तेरा पर प्रेम पिलावै भंग । जाके अमल दरश ह्वै हरि को नैनन आवै रंग ।।

उनके चरण शरणहीं लागो सेवा करो उमंग । चरणदास तिनको पग परशन आशा करत है गंग ।।

६ ईश्वर महिमा

दोहा

बिन होनी हरि करिकै, होनी देहिं मिटाय।
चरणदास करु भक्तिही, आपा देहु उठाय ॥७९॥
हरि चितवै सो सांची बाता। औरनसौं नहिं टूटै पाता ॥
जो कछु चाहा सो उन करई। अब चाहै सो भी सब सरई ॥
अग्नि माहिं तृण घास बस बचावै। घट में सगरो सिंधु समावै ॥
पावक राखै पानी माहीं। जल राखै जहँ धरती नाहीं ॥
गिरिवर सागर माहिं तरावै। चाहै हलका काठ डुबावै ॥
सुइ के नोके हस्ती काढै। मूल पांत बिन लकडी बाढै ॥
नरकी छाती दूध निकासै। उपजावै वह खेत अकासै ॥
चाहै गूँगे वेद पढावैं। अँधरे आँखें खोलि दिखावैं ॥
सब लायक समरत्थ गुसाँई। चरणदास शुकदेव बताई ॥

दोहा

प्रभु चाहै सोई करे, ताकूँ टोकै कौन।
देखि देखि अचरज रहा, चरणदास गहि मौन ॥८०॥
महल पवनपर रचै मुरारी। अग्निके माहिं करै फुलवारी ॥
चाहै बिन बादल बरसावै। बिन सूरज दिन करि दिखलावै ॥
खाली भरै भरे निघटावै। जो चाहै सोइ प्रगटावै ॥
पाथर पानी करै बहावै। छिन में सगरो सिंधु सुखावै ॥
चाहै जलका थल करि डारै। राई कूं परबत करि भारै ॥
रंकन कूं करै छत्तर धारी। चाहै भूपन देइ उजारी ॥
जो चाहै सो आपहि करैं। औरनके शिर झूठे धरैं ॥
चरणदास शुकदेव जनावै। सांचे गुणावाद जो गावै ॥

दोहा

यह अस्तुति करतार की, जिन रचिया संसार ।
अद्भुत कौतक करि रह्यो, लीला अगम अपार ।।८१।।
उपजावै पालै विनशावै । अनगिन चन्द सूर दरशावै ।।
कोटिक अंड पलक में करै । जब चाहै तब कुछ ना रहै ।।
जब फैले तब रूप अनेका । जब समिटै तब एकहि एका ।।
वटके बीजका खेलनहारा । एक बीजका सकल पसारा ।।
तामें बीज अनंतहि देखा । गिनूं कहां लौं रंग न रेखा ।।
ऐसे हरि आपा विस्तारा । कहत सुनत देखतहूं हारा ।।
अपरंपार पार नहिं पाऊं । अस्तुति करता मैं सकुचाऊं ।।
समझि समझि मन में रहि जाऊं । चरणदास हो शीश नवाऊं ।।

दोहा

लीला सिंधु अगाध गति, मो पै कही न जाय ।
चरणदास यों कहत है, शोचत गयो हिराय ।।८२।।
कोटिक ब्रह्मा अस्तुति करहीं । वेद कहत प्रभु परे परेहीं ।।
कोटिक शम्भू करैं समाधा । जानि परै नहिं रूप अगाधा ।।
कोटिक नारद से यश गावैं । गुण अगाध कछु अन्त न पावैं ।।
कोटिक ध्यानी ध्यान लगावैं । हरि के सो कछु रूप न पावैं ।।
कोटिक ज्ञानी कथैं वह ज्ञाना । समझ थकी उनहूं नहिं जाना ।।
कोटिक शारद करैं विचारा । बुद्धि थकी जब कहा अपारा ।।
सुर नर मुनि वा भेद न लहिया । शोचि शोचि बकि बकि थकिरहिया ।।
निरगुण सरगुण कहा न जावै । चरणदास शुकदेव सुनावै ।।

दोहा

चरणदास वा रूपकी, पटतर दई न जाइ ।
राम सरीखे राम हैं, और बताऊं काइ ।।८३।।
वाकी अस्तुति कहां बखानूं । जैसा वह तैसा नहिं जानूं ।।
बूधि विचार करि हारा ज्ञाना । अनभै थकी नाहिं पहिंचाना ।।
आदि न अन्त मध्य नहिं जाका । दहिना बाँया पीठ न आका ।।
हरा पीत पुनि श्वेत न काला । नारी पुरुष न बूढा बाला ।।
रूप न रंग मिहीं नहिं मोटा । नया पुराना बड़ा न छोटा ।।

नाम रूप करिया सूं न्यारा । नहिं हलका नहिं कहिये भारा ।।
वानी चार पर निरवाना । काहू विधि वह जाय न जाना ।।
पुष्प गंध नादन तैं झीना । गुरु शुकदेव सुनाय जु दीना ।।

दोहा
कौन लखै को कहि सकै, अचरज अलख अभेव ।
ज्ञान ध्यान पहुँचै नहीं, निर्विकार निर्लेव ।।८४।।
सुनत अचम्भा मोकूं आया । जाके वचन रूप नहिं काया ।।
निराकार नहिं ना आकारा । नहिं अडोल नहिं डोलन हारा ।।
पांच तत्त्व त्रैगुण ते आगे । अद्‌भुत अचरज ध्यान न लागे ।।
नहिं परगट नहिं गूप न ठाऊं । समझ सकूं नहिं थकि थकि जाऊं ।।
जैसो आगे मैं कहि आयो । फिर समझो वैसो नहिं पायो ।।
जो कुछ कहिया नाहीं नाहीं । सो सब देखा वाके माहीं ।।
सकल सर्वदा ह्वां पहिचानी । चरणदास शुकदेव बखानी ।।

दोहा
वामें गुण अनगिनत हैं, अपरंपार अगाध ।
देखौ परगटही भये, रूप नाम अरु नाद ।।८५।।
वृक्ष बीजका भेद बताऊं । भिन्न भिन्न परगट दिखलाऊं ।।
जो कोइ निरा बीजकूं बूझै । ताकूं वह निर्गुणही सूझै ।।
जब समझ तब सब गुण माहीं । तामें डाल मूल फल छाहीं ।।
ऐसे पूरण ब्रह्म पिछानौ । निराकार निर्गुण मत जानौ ।।
वे निर्गुण सरगुण ते न्यारे । निर्गुण सरगुण नाम विचारो ।।
अकथ कथा कछु कथिय न जाई । जो भाषू सोई मुरखाई ।।
कोई कहौ सुनौ मन आनौ । वैसा नहिं निश्चय करि जानौ ।।
बड बड ऋषि मुनि पंडित भारे । चरणदास सब खोजत हारे ।।

दोहा
वहि निर्गुण सरगुण वही, वही दोइसे न्यार ।
जो था सो जाना नहीं।। शोबारम्बार चा ।। ८६।।
अनन्त सकल लीला अनंत, गुण अनन्त बहु भाव ।
कौतुक रूप अनंत हैं, चरणदास बलि जाव।।८७।।

नामभेदअनंत करिया, धर अनंत अवतार।
बीस चार तिनमें अधिक, कहै शुकदेव विचार ।।८८।।
राम कृष्ण पूरण कला, चौबीसों में होय।
निरगुण से सरगुण वही, भक्तों कारण दोय ।।८९।।

राग बिलावल
अलख निरंजन अगम अपर।
एक अनेक भेष बहु कीन्हे सुन्दर रचना रची सँवार ।।
निरगुण हरि सरगुण हो खेलो अचरज लीना करि विस्तार।
अपनो चरित आपही देखे ऐसो अद्भुत कौतुक धार ।।
रूप वराह पकरि हिरण्याक्षहि धरती लाये ताहि सिधार।
यक्ष पुरुष अरु दत्तात्रेयी अरु श्रीबद्रीपतिही विचार ।।
सनत्कुमार ॠषभदेव बधू वराह पृथू मच्छ कूर्म उदार।
हयग्रीव अरु हंस रूपही महाबली नरसिंह बलधार ।।
हरि परगट ह्वै छुटायो वामन कपिल सरस गुणसार।
मन्वन्तर धन्वन्तर प्रगटे परशुराम रामचन्द्र मुरार।
पूरण कलाईस तिहुँ पुरको कृष्ण प्रगट हो कंस पछार ।।
वेदव्यास अरु बोध कलंकी ये भये सब चौबीस अवतार ।।
युग युग माहिं आप परगट ह्वै दुष्ट दलन सन्तन रखवार।
चरणदास शुकदेव श्याम की बाँकी गति को वार न पार ।।

दोहा
एक एक सों आगरो, महिमा कही न जाय।
अनन्त रँगीले महल में, आपहि बैठे आय ।।९० ।।
अनन्त रँगीले महल बनाये। तामें आप रामही आये ।।
राम रूप गुण न्यारे न्यारे। गिनत शारदा गणपति हारे ।।
मन्दिर रूप बहुत छबि सोहै। जहाँ तहाँ मेरा मन मोहै ।।
हरियर श्वेत पीत अरु लाले। पिसताकी ऊदै अरु काले ।।
बेलदार लहरा छबि बूटे। चीतमताले और तिखूंटे ।।
बूँद बूँद अवगंडे दारे। जानौ चित्तर हाय संवारे ।।
रँग रँग बहु चित्तकारी। कहूं कहाँ लौ मौ बुधिहारी ।।
दो पायें अरु पुनि चौपाये। बहु पाये कछु कहे न जाये ।।

वृक्षरूप अरु पक्षी नाना। कीट पतंगा थिर चर जाना ।।
जल में मीन बहुत परकारे। चरणदास शुकदेव विचारे ।।

दोहा
थावर जंगम चर अचर, बहुत छबीली भाँति।
राजस तामस सात्विकी, बहु अधीन बहु क्रांति ।।९१।।
वानर नर असुरा सुरा, यक्षगण गन्धर्व प्रेत।
सबही महल बराबरी, सबही सेती हेत ।।९२।।
खिरकी नैन चाव सों खोलै। मुख द्वारे नाना विधि बोलै ।।
बहुत भाँति की नाना बानी। चतुर कूट भोली अरु यानी ।।
कहिं अबोल बोल न आवै। पै सब महलन वह दरशावै ।।
साक्षात हरिही कूं जानै। भवन भवन में ताहि पिछानै ।।
काया क्षेतर ज्ञानी जानै। क्षेत्रज्ञ आतम रूप बखानै ।।
देही क्षर गीता में गायो। अक्षर जीव खोल दिखलायो ।।
काया मन्दिर आप रमायो। ताते राम नाम धरवायो ।।
देह सँयोग राम कहलायो। चरणदास शुकदेव बतायो ।।

दोहा
सूरज चींटी आदि दै, लघु दीरध के माहिं ।।
सबमें पोई आतमा, बाहर कोई नाहिं ।।९३।।
छोटे भांडे में करै, छोटाही परकाश।
बड जू भांडे में करै, ज्यादा होय उकाश ।।९४।।
ज्ञानवन्त कूं मैं दियो, दीपक को दृष्टान्त।
जो वह समझै चाव सूं, मिटै तिमिर अरु भ्रान्त ।।९५।।
जैसेही है पिण्ड में, तैसेही ब्रह्मण्ड।
भीतर बाहर रमि रह्यो, सात द्वीप नव खण्ड ।।९६।।
आप लखेते वाकूं पावै। जो पै सद्गुरु भेद बतावै ।।
ज्ञान दृष्टी सेती दरशावै। आपा मिटै ब्रह्म ठहरावै ।।
ज्ञाता ज्ञान ज्ञेय जहँ नाहीं। ध्याता ध्यान ध्येय मिटि जाहीं ।।
जब हो एक दूसरा नासे। बन्ध मुकत के रहै न साँसै ।।
मृतक अवस्था जीवत आवै। करम रहित अस्थिर गति पावै ।।

तब कोइ मिन्तर वैरी नाहीं। पाप पुण्य की परै न छाहीं ।।
हर्ष शोक सम हो जा दोऊ। रक्षा करो कि मारो कोऊ ।।
कोउ हाथ में भोजन दे जा। कोउ छीनकर याहीं ले जा ।।
दोनों एक बराबर वाके। जग ब्योहार कछू नहिं जाके ।।
हरि बिन और पिछान न कोई। तिनके इच्छा रही न दोई ।।
ज्ञान दिशा ऐसे करि गाई। चरणदास शुकदेव बताई ।।

दोहा
ज्ञान दिशा आवन कठिन, विरला जानै कोय।
ज्ञान दिशा जब जानिये, जीवत मृत्यक दोय ।।९७।।

७ वाचक ज्ञानी

वाचक ज्ञानी बहुतक देखे । ज्ञानी लक्ष कोइ लेखे लेखे ।।
ज्ञानी बिगडै विषयी होई । कथा एक अरु चालै दोई ।।
बुरे करम औगुण चित लावै । भले करम गुण सब बिसरावै ।।
विषय वासना के रग रातो । झूठ कपट छल बल मदमातो ।।
इन्द्री वश मन हाथ न आवै । पाप करन सों नाहिं डरावै ।।
ज्ञान कथै अरु बाद बढावै । रहन गहन का भेद पावै ।।
ब्रह्म व्रत का आवन भारी । चरणदास शुकदेव विचारी ।।

दोहा
उनतीसों लक्षण लिये। ज्ञान को सहत भक्त ,
ज्ञान दिशा जब आय है ध्यान आतमा करै ,।।९८।।

८ नवधा भक्ति

दोहा

भक्ति दिशा अब कहत है, बिसरै आपा आप।
चरणदास यों कहत है, छूटैं तीनों ताप ॥९९॥

अष्टपदी

नवधा भक्ति सँभारि अंग नौ जानिले। श्रवणन चिंतन और कीर्त्तन मानिले ॥
सुमिरण वन्दन ध्यान और पूजा करो। प्रभु सों प्रीति लगाय सुरति चरणन धरो ॥
हो करि दासहि भाव साध संगति रलो। भक्तन की सेव यही मत है भलो ॥
आपा अर्पण देय धीर्य्य दृढता गहौ। क्षमा शील संतोष दया धारे रहो ॥
यह जो मैंने कहा वेद का फूल है। योग ज्ञान वैराग्य सबन का मूल है ॥
प्रेमा भक्ति का तात पात तीनों नसैं। धर्म अर्थ काम मोक्ष सकल तामें वसैं ॥
जो राखै मन माहिं विवेक विचार सों। पावै पद निर्वाण बचै जग भार सों ॥
कहै गुरु शुकदेव माया के भाव सों। चरणहिं दासा होय सुनौ बहु चाव सों ॥

राग सोरठ

वा गौरी वा आसावरी

साधो नवधा भक्ति करो रे। कलियुग में यह बडो पदारथ गहि गहि ताहि तरो रे॥
जे जे यासों भये शिरोमणि तिनको नाम सुनाऊं। बढै कथा विस्तारै कहूँ तो याते सूक्षम गाऊं ॥
जन प्रहलाद तरो सुमिरण ते वंदन सों अक्रर। चरणकमल की सेवा सेती लक्ष्मी रहत हजूर ॥
चन्दन चर्चत हूं पृथुराजा उतरो भवजल पार। बलि राजा तन अर्पण कीन्हों सदा रहै हरिद्वार ॥परमदास हनुमत हूं उबरो उत्तम पदवी पाई। सखा सुभाव तरो है अर्जुन ताकी महिमा गाई ॥

मुक्त भयो है परीक्षित राजा सुन भागवत पुराना । श्रीशुकदेव मुनी से वक्ता हुए रूप भगवाना ।।ज्ञान योग वैराग्य सबन सों प्रेम प्रीति है न्यारी । चरणदासने गुरु किरपा सों सांची बात बिचारी ।।

९ प्रेमा भक्ति

दोहा

नवो अंग के साध ते, उपजै प्रेम अनूप ।
रणजीता यों जानिये, सब धर्मन का भूप ।।१००।।
सब मत अधिकी प्रेम बतावै । योग युगत सूं बडा दिखावै ।।
प्रेमहिं सूं उपजे वैरागा । प्रेमहिं सूं उपजै मन त्यागा ।।
प्रेम भक्ति सूं उपजै ज्ञाना । होय चांदना मिटै अज्ञाना ।।
दुर्लभ प्रेम जु हाथ न आवै । हरि किरपा करि दे तौ पावै ।।
प्रेम प्रीति के वश भगवाना । सकल शास्ती कियौ बखाना ।।
किसी भक्ति हिय प्रेम जु जागे । तौ हरि दरशत रहै जु आगे ।।
प्रेमहिं सूं जग कूं उहजावै । निर्गुण सर्गुण हो हो आवै ।।
सकल शिरोमणि प्रेमहि जानौ । चरणदास निहचै मन आनौ ।।

दोहा

प्रेम बराबर योग ना, प्रेम बराबर ज्ञान ।
प्रेम भक्ति बिन साधिवो, सबही थोथा ध्यान ।।१०१।।
प्रेम छुटावै जगत कूं, प्रेम मिलावै राम ।
प्रेम गति औरही, लै पहुँचै हरिधाम ।।१०२।।
वह करै काग सूं हंसा । एक रहै पियाका संसा ।।
वह जात बरन कुल खोवै । अरु बीज विरह का बोवै ।।
जो प्रेम तनक चित आवै । वह औगुण सबै नशावै ।।
प्रेम लता जब लहरैं । मन बिना योगही ठहरैं ।।
कोई चतुर खिलारी खेलै । वह प्रेम पियाला झेलै ।।
जो धडपै शीश न राखै । सोई प्रेम पियाला चाखै ।।
तन मन सूं जो बौराई । वह रहै ध्यान लौलाइ ।।
वह पहुँचै हरिकै पासा । यों कहैं चरणही दासा ।।

दोहा

प्रेमी जन हरि आप हो, आपा निकसे नाहिं ।
गुरु शुकदेव दिखावई, समझ देखि मन माहिं ।।१०३।।
हिरदे माहीं प्रेम जो, नैनौं झलकै आय ।
सोइ छका हरिरस पगा, वा पग परसो धाय ।।१०४।।
गदगद बाणी कंठ में, आँशू टपके नैन ।
वह तो विरहिनि रामकी, तलफत है दिन रैन ।।१०५।।
हाय हाय हरि कब मिलै, छाती फाती जाय ।
ऐसा दिन कब होयगा, दर्शन करै अघाय ।।१०६।।
बिन दर्शन कल ना पडै, मनुआँ धरै न धीर ।
चरणदास की श्याम बिन, कौन मिटावै पीर ।।१०७।।
पीव बिना ना जीवना, जग में भारी जान ।
पिया मिलै तो जीवना, नहिं तौ छूटै प्रान ।।१०८।।
मुख पियरो सूखै अधर, आँखें खरी उदास ।
आहि जु निकसै दुख भरी, गहिरे लेत उसाँस ।।१०९।।
वह विरहिनि बौरी भई, जानता ना कोइ भेद ।
अगिनी बैर हियरा जरै, भये कलेजे छेद ।।११०।।
अपने वश वह ना रही, फँसी विरह के जाल ।
चरणदास रोवत रहै, सुमिरि सुमिरि गुण ख्याल ।।१११।।
बातन को विरह लगो, ज्यों घुन लागो दार ।
दिन दिन पीरी होत है, पिया न बूझे सार ।।११२।।
वैनहिं बूझैं सारही, बिरहिनि कौन हवाल ।
जब सुधि आवै लाल की, चुभत कलेजे भाल ।।११३।।
पीव चहौ कै मत चहौ, वहतौ पीकी दास ।
पिय के रंग राती रहै, जग सो होय उदास ।।११४।।
पीपी करते दिन गया, रैनि गई पिय ध्यान ।
विरहिनिके सहजैं सधै, भक्ति योग अरु ज्ञान ।।११५।।
विरहिनि एकै राम विन, और न कोई मीत ।
आठ पहर साठौ घड़ी, पिया मिलन की चीत ।।११६।।
जाप करै तौ पीव का, ध्यान करै तो पीव ।
पीव विरहिनि का जीव है, जीविरहिनि कापीव।।११७।।

१० चारोंयुगवर्णन

सतयुग

कुंडलिया

सतयुग सांचा बोलते, परमहंस को ध्यान।
सतवादी सत राखते, सत नहिं देते जान ।।
सत नहिं देते जान, प्राल जो पै तजि देही।
निश्चय होती मुक्ति, दरशते राम सनेही ।।
शुकदेव यही चरणदास सों, अबही सतयुग जान।
संत बोले सत सों रहो, सत की गहियो आन ।।१।।

त्रेता

त्रेता में तप साधते, आसन संयम धार।
पांचौं इन्द्री रोकते, जब मन जाता हार ।।
जब मन जाता हार, खैंचि अनहद में धरते।
कै अपनोही इष्ट ध्यान ताही को धरते।
आप विसर्जन होय मुक्ति निश्चय कर पाते।
चरणदास शुकदेव तपस्या चाल दिखाते ।।२।।

द्वापर

कुं परद्वा पूजा वंदन, प्रेमसहित जो होय
कहा राजसी मानसी पूजा कहिये दोय ।।
पूजा कहिये दोय जैसी जाकै मन भावै।
धारै नेम अचार डलावै चित्त ना अंत ।।
हित करि पूजा कीजिये। भेव यह को द्वापर,
चरणदास निश्चय करो कहिया श्री शुकदेव ।।३ ।।

कलियुग

कलियुग हरिगुण गाइये गुणवादही सार,
भजन करो मन मगन ह्वैनिवार सकुच अरु भय ।।
भय अरु सकुच निवार। बहावो गर्व कुल जाति , साज बाज लै रंग गाय को राम ,
रिझावो।।
कथा कीरतन सो तरैमाहिं। के कलियुगही , शुकदेव कहि चरणदास सों तारों ,
गहि गहि बाहिं ।।४।।

११ अथ अंग नाम बर्णन

दोहा

प्रणऊं श्री शुकदेव कूं बाणी कहूं अगाध ।
महिमा गाऊं नाम की सब मिलि सुनियो साध ।।११।।११८।।
ज्योंकी त्योंहीं कहत हूं कछू न राखूं भेद ।।
निश्चय आवै नाम की छूटै सबही खेद ।।२।।११९।।
जनम मरन मयदंड के गर्भ बास की त्रास ।
नाम रटे सबही छूटै लख चौरासी गास ।।३।।१२०।।
कई बार जो यज्ञ करि योग करै चितलाय ।।
चरणदास कहैं नाम बिन सखी अकालहि जाय ।।४।।१२१।।
आठ धात मैं गुण नहीं जो पारस के माहिं ।।
तप तीरथ ब्रत साधना राम नाम सम नाहिं ।।५।।१२२।।
ज्यों सेमर का सेवना ज्यों लोभी का धर्म्म ।।
अन्न बिना भुस कूटना नाम बिना यों कर्म्म।।६।।१२३।।
छोड़ै सबही बासना हो बैठै निष्काम ।।
चरण कमल मैं चित धरै सुमिरै रामहिं राम ।।७।।१२४।।
ऐसा हो जब संत हो तब रीझै करतार ।।
दरशन दे अपना करै कभी न छोड़ै लार ।।८।।१२५।।
चार वेद किये व्यास ने अर्थ बिचार बिचार ।।
तामें निकसे भक्तिही राम नाम ततसार ।।९।।१२६।।
जिन कहिया शुकदेव कूं सुनिया प्रेम प्रतीति ।।
तिन जग में परगट कियो जैसी चहिये रीति ।।१०।।१२७।।
ब्रह्महत्या अरु नारि की बालक हत्या होय ।।
राम नाम जो मन बसै सब कूं डारै खोय ।।११।।१२८।।
हिय आवत जग दुख टरै कंठ आय अघ जाय ।।
मुख सूं बोलै आयकरि ताकी कौन चलाय ।।१२।।१२९।।
ऐसाही हरिनामहीं मोहिं रामकी सौहिं ।।
जाकूं होवै परखही सो समझै ह्यां लौहिं ।।१३।।१३०।।

बिन समझे पातक नशैं मुक्त हो जपै समझ ॥
चरणदास यों कहत हैं जो कोइ जानै युक्त ॥१४॥१३१॥
नामहिं लै जल पीजिये नामहिं लेकरि खाह ॥
नामहिं लेकरि बैठिये नामहिं लै चल राह ॥१५॥१३२॥
जब लग जागै राम कहु तन मन सूं यहि चीत ॥
चरणदास यों कहत हैं हरि बिन और न मीत ॥१६॥१३३॥
तेरा तौ कोइ है नहीं मात पिता सुत नार ॥
ताते सुमिरौ राम कूं हे मन बारम्बार ॥१७॥१३४॥
जिहि कारण भटकत फिरै घर घर करत सलाम ॥
तेरे तौ वै हैं नहीं ये मन सुमिरौ राम ॥१८॥१३५॥
जीवतही स्वारथ लगै मूये देह जराय ॥
ऐ मन सुमिरो राम कूं धोखे काहि पराय ॥१९॥१३६॥
हाथी घोड़े धन घना चंदमुखी बहु नार ॥
नाम बिना यमलोक में पावे दुःख अपार ॥२०॥१३७॥
जबलग जीवै राम कहु रामहिं सेती नेह ॥
जीव मिलैगो राम में पड़ी रहैगी देह ॥२१॥१३८॥
अचरज साधन नामका भक्ति योग का जीव ॥
जैसै दूध जमाय कै मथि करि काढ़ा घीव ॥२२॥१३९॥

कुंडलिया

आठ मास मुखसूं जपै सोलह मास कँठ जाप । बतिस मास हिरदै जपै तन में रहै न पाप ॥

तन में रहै न पाप भक्ति का उपजै पौधा । मन रुक जावै जहां अपरबल कहिये योधा ॥

शुकदेन कही चरणदास सूं यही भेद ततसार । बिहुरू आवै नाभि में ताका कहूं बिचार ॥२३॥

दोहा

पाँच बरष जप नाभि सों रगरग बोले राम ॥
देह जीव निज भक्त हो पहुँचे हरिके धाम ॥२४॥१४०॥
त्रिकुटी में जप राम कूं जहां उजाला होय ॥

श्वासा माहीं जपेते द्विविधा रहै न कोय ॥१५॥१४१॥
गगन मँडल में जापकरि जित है दशवां द्वार ॥
चरणदास यों कहत हैं सो पहुँचै हरि दरबार ॥२६॥१४२॥
नासा अग्रे जाप करि देखै नूर अगाध ॥
बहुतक अचरज अरु खुलै चरणदास कहैं साध ॥२७॥१४३॥
नाम उठाकर नाभि सूं गगन माहिं लै जाय ॥
जहाँ होय परकाशही शुकदेव दिया बताय ॥२८॥१४४॥
मनही मनमें जाप करि दर्पण उज्ज्वल होय ॥
दर्शन हौवै राम का तिमिर जाय सब खोय ॥२९॥१४५॥
कूककूक कर नाम जप छुटै सात अरु पांच ॥
जासों मन ठहरा रहै चरणदास कहैं साँच ॥३०॥१४६॥
सुरत माहिं जो जप करै तन सूं न्यारा जौन ॥
मिलै सच्चिदानन्द में गहे रहै जो मौन ॥३१॥१४७॥
सकल शिरोमणि नाम है सब धर्मन के माहिं ॥
अनन्य भक्त वहि जानिये सुमिरण भूलै नाहिं ॥३२॥१४८॥
आन धरम मानै नहीं आनदेव नहिं ध्यान ॥
ऐसे भक्त अनन्य कूं कोई पावै जान ॥३३॥१४९॥
पतिब्रता वह जानिये अज्ञा करै न भंग ॥
पिय अपने के रँग रतै और न सूनै ढंग ॥३४॥१५०॥
अपने पिय कूं सेइये आन पुरुष तजि देह ॥
पर घर नेह निवारिये रहिये अपने गेह ॥३५॥१५१॥
आज्ञाकारी पीवकी रहै पिया के संग ॥
तन मन सूं सेवा करै और न दूजो रंग ॥३६॥१५२॥
रंग होय तौ पीव को आन पुरुष विषरूप ॥
छाहँबुरी पर घरन की अपनी भलीजु धूप ॥३७॥१५३॥
भलीजु अपने घर का दुख भला परघरका सुख छार ॥
ऐसे जानै कुलबधू सो सतवन्ती नार ॥३८॥१५४॥
पति की ओर निहारिये औरन से कह काम ॥
सबै देवता छोड़करि जपिये हरि का नाम ॥३९॥१५५॥
खसम तुम्हारो राम है इत उत रुख मतमारि ॥
चरणदास यों कहत हैं यही धारणा धारि ॥४०॥१५६॥
यह शिरनवै तो रामकूं नाहीं गिरियो टूट ॥

आनदेव नहिं परसिये यह तन जावो छूट ॥४१॥१५७॥
पतिब्रता को ब्रत गहौ ब्यभिचारिणि अँग टार ॥
पतिपावै सब दुख नशैं पावै सुक्ख अपार ॥४२॥१५८॥
जब तू जानै पीवही वह अपनो करि लेहि ॥
परम धाम में राखि करि बांह पकरि सुख देहि ॥४३॥१५९॥
यही सिखापन देतहूं धारो हिरदय माहिं ॥
ऐसा पौधा बोइये ताकी बैठे छाहिं ॥४४॥१६०॥
सतबादी सत सूं रहो सतही मुख सूं बोल ॥
एक ओर हरि नाम रख एक ओर जग तोल ॥४५॥१६१॥
सभी निचोरे कहत हूं भक्ति करी निष्काम ॥
कोटि तपस्या यही है मुख सूं कहिये राम ॥४६॥१६२॥
राम नाम मुख सुं कहै राम नाम सुन कान ॥
रोम रोम हरि कूं रटो ऐसी गहिये बान ॥४७॥१६३॥
विद्या माहीं वाद है तपके माहीं ऋद्धि ॥
राम नाम में मुक्ति है योग माहिं यों सिद्धि ॥४८॥१६४॥
ताते त्यागो बासना राखो रामहिं नाम ॥
कोटि बन्ध छुटि जायँगे पहुँचौ हरि के धाम ॥४९॥१६५॥
राम नाम ये सबै ऋद्धि सिद्धि औ मोक्ष ॥
ऐसा इष्ट सँभारिये चरणदास कहि सोक्ष ॥५०॥१६६॥
सोच जाका कीया सब बना सात द्वीप नवखण्ड ॥
चरणदास यों कहत है तीन लोक ब्रह्मण्ड ॥५१॥१६७॥
तव कारण सब कुछ किया नाना विधि सुखदीन ॥
तैं वाकूं जाना नहीं नाम न कबहूं लीन ॥५२॥१६८॥
अब कै औसर फिरि बन्यो पाई मानुष देह ॥
बन्यो चरणदास यों कहत हैं राम नामहीं लेह ॥५३॥१६९॥

राग केदारा

सुनौ भाई नामकी महीमा ।
मुक्ति चारौं सिद्धि आठौं बसत हैं तहि मा ॥
बालमीक सो बनके बासी किये थे जिन पाप ॥
भयो है सब ऋषि शिरोमणि जपो उलटो जाप ॥

गणिका सी अति महापापी सो पढ़ावत कीर ।।
नामके परताप सेती कियो हरि पुर सीर ।।
अजामील से पतित कामी बेश्या सों रति कीन ।।
चढ़ि बिमानै गयो सुरपुर नाम सुत हित लीन ।।
और बहुतै पतित तारे गिने कापै जाहिं ।।
दान जप तप योग संयम नाम सम तुल नाहिं ।।
ब्यास नारद शिव ब्रह्मादिक रटत जाकूं शेश ।।
गुरु शुकदेव नामको चरणदास कूं उपदेश ।।५४।।

कवित्त

नाम के प्रताप नन्दलाल आप भये प्रभु
नाम के प्रताप सुत दशरथ को कहायो है ।।
नाम के प्रताप पैज राखी प्रहलादजू की
नाम के प्रताप दौरो द्वारका सूं धायो है ।।
नाम के प्रताप की न महिमा मोपै कही जात
नाम के प्रताप सब सन्तन सहायो है ।।
सोई नाम बास अब आस लगो चरणदास सोई
नाम चार वेद विमल विमल गायो है ।।५५।।
नाम के प्रताप शबरी सुरनतैं सरस करी
नाम के प्रताप अधम लोक कूं पठायो है ।।
नाम के प्रताप अजामील कूं विमान आयो
नाम के प्रताप गज ग्राह सूं छुटायो है ।।
नाम के प्रताप सब दीननको दुःख हरो
नाम को प्रताप शुकदेवजी दृढायो है ।।
सोई नाम बास अब आस लगो चरणदास
सोई नाम चार वेद विमल विमल गायो है ।।५६।।

दोहा

नाम अंग महिमा अधिक मोहै कही न जाय ।।
पांच प्रेत अब कहत हूं जाकूं सुनि चितलाय ।।१७०।।

१२ वर्णन प्रेत पंच

योग तपस्या भक्ति कूं ज्ञान बिगाड़न पांच ॥
जीवत दुख दै जगत में मुये नरक दै आंच ॥५८॥१७१॥
काम क्रोध मोह लोभ से और पाँचवां गर्ब्ब ॥
राज करै बसुधा बिषे इन बश कीने सर्ब्ब ॥५९॥१७२॥
काम बली बर्णन करूं जिन मारे बलवन्त ॥
जाका बकसी नारि है जीते गुणी महन्त ॥६०॥१७३॥

[नारी वर्णन] राग सोरठ
साधो नारि सबल रे भाई। नहिं मानै राम दुहाई ॥
बांदर ज्यों पकरि नचावै। हरिजी सूं नेह छुटावै ॥
दया धर्म सब खोवै। जब नैन कजल भरि जोवै ॥
जिनका चित चोरा रांड़ी। तिनकी जग थू थू भांड़ी ॥
उन सबही सरबस खोया। नर शीश पकरि करि रोया ॥
जनम पदारथ छीना। स्याही का टीका दीना ॥
दोनों मुख सों खाया। फिर फिरकै गरभ दिखाया ॥
काम कटक मैं सूरी। वह साँवत कहिये पूरी ॥
बड़े बड़े योधा मारे। अरु बहुतक शूर पछारे ॥
गुरु शुकदेव बतावै। बटमारन तोहिं दिखावै ॥
चरणदास यह जानौ। तुम छलबल कला पिछानौ ॥६१॥१७४॥
नारी नैहरि सुमरण सूँ खोये। राजा परजा मुंडत चुंडत नैन कटाक्षन मोहे ॥
चुंडत राती चूनर चटक मटक ले भूषण का काजल साधै ॥
मुख मुसकावै मधुरी वानी प्यार प्रीत कर बांधै ॥
बहुतन को उन योग छुटायो बहुतन का तप छीनों ॥
बहुतनकी उन भक्ति बिगारी अंग विषय रस दीन्हों ॥
बहुवां करि बहु नाच नचायो फंदा मोह लगायो ॥
बहुवां याते सावधानही रहियो मैं तुम कूं समुझायो ॥

गुरु शुकदेव बतावै साधो निश्चय ठगिनी जानौ ।।
चरणदास कहैं हाथ न आवो नीके ताहि पिछानौ ।।६२।।
साधौ पर तिरिया सूं डरियो ।
जाके दरश परष के कीये जीवत नरक में परियो ।।
गौतम घरनी सुन्दरि सुनिकै इन्द्रासन तजि आयो ।
जो गति भई जगत मैं जानी भलौ कलंक लगायो ।।
शृङ्गी ऋषि बन में तप कीन्हो सुरपति देखि डरायो ।
रंभा भेजि हरो सत जाको सबही सेज सिरायो ।।
दैवत देवत नर जो हूये नारी देख लुभाये ।
ताको फल ऐसोही पायो अजहूं कुयश सुनाये ।।
चरणदास शुकदेव गुरु ने दे उपदेश बचाये ।
यती सती कोइ हाथ न आयो कामी पकरि नचाये ।।६३।।
अरे नर परनारी मत तक रे ।
जिन जिन ओर तको डायन की बहुतन कूं गई भख रे ।।
दूध आक को पात कटइया झाल अँगन की जानौ ।
सिंह मुछारे बिषकारे को ऐसे ताहि पिछानौ ।।
खानि नरक की अति दुख बाई चौरासी भरमावै ।
जनम जनम कूं दाग लगावै हरिगुरु तुरत छुटावै।।
जग में फिरि फिरि महिमा खोवै राखै तन मन मैला ।
चरणदास शुकदेव चितावै सुमिरो राम सुहेला ।।६४।।

दोहा
नरनारी सब चेतियो दीन्हो प्रगट दिखाय ।।
पर तिरिया पर पुरुषहो भोग नरक को जांय ।।६५।।१७४।।
पर नारी कै आपनी दोनों बुरी बलाय ।।
घर बाहर की आग ज्यों देवै हाथ जलाय ।।६६।।१७५।।

काम जीतन के उपाय
दोहा
चटक मटक सब छोड दे देही रूप बिगार ।
देख न कोई रीझि हैं ना होवे लगवार ।।६७।।१७६।।

यही ढाल है जस्त की लगै न शस्ती काम ।
आठ अंग हैं काम के तासूं रहु निष्काम ।।६८।।१७७।।
काम कान में आय करि फिर आवत है नैन ।।
बहुरि हिये आय करि लगै बहुत दुख दैन ।।६९।।१७८।।

चौपई
वह काम बुरा रे भाई । सब देवै तन बौराई ।।
पंचौं में नाक कटावै । वह जुती मार दिलावै ।।
मुँह काला गधे चढ़ावै । बहु लोग तमाशे आवैं ।।
कुत्ता झिड़का ज्यों डोलै कूता । सबही के मन सूं ऊता ।।
कोई नीके मुख नहिं बोलै । शरमिंदा हो जग में डोलै ।।
वह जीवत नरक मँझारी । सुन चेतौ नर अरु नारी ।।
काम अंग तजि दीजै । सतसंगतिही करि लीजै ।।
कहैं स्वामि चरण हीं दासा । हरि भक्तन में कर बासा ।।७०।।१७९।।

दोहा
तन मन जारै काम हीं चित करै डावांडोल ।।
धरम करम सब खोय कै रहै आप हिय खोल ।।७१।।१८०।।

चौपई
वह दया क्षमा को मारै । जत सत को पकरि पछारै ।।
शुचि नेम को दूरि कढ़ावै । मुख ऊपर धूरि उड़ावै ।।
जग भीतर महीमा खोवै । पापों की माला पोवै।।
वह धीरज नाहीं राखै । वह मुख सों झूठी भाखै ।।
वह चाल चलै बिपरीता । करि बिषय भोग की चीता ।।
काम बली जहँ आवै । अरु बहुतक औगुण लावै ।।
यह मैन खोट का पूरा । कोइ जीतै गुरुमुख शूरा ।।
मैन साधु भक्ति वही गुनियां । जिन काम दुष्ट को हनिया ।।
चेत कही शुकदेवा । सब चरणदास सुनिलेवा ।।७२।।१८१।।

दोहा

सुनि कै जो चित में धरै फेरि चलै वह चाल ।।
खांड़ा पकरै शील का काम हनै ततकाल ।।७३।।१८२।।

दोहा

क्रोध महा चंडाल है जानत है सब कोय ।।
जाके अंग बरणन करूं सुनियो सुरति समोय ।।१८१।।
क्रोध भूत के चरित सुनाऊं । भिन्न भिन्न परगट दिखलाऊं ।।
क्रोध भूत जब तापर आवै । तन मन की सब सुधि बिसरावै ।।
नैना लाल बदन सब कारो । रोम रोम व्यापौ हत्यारो ।।
महा चंडाल नीच अति घोरी । अति बिपरीत बुद्धि करि औरी ।।
अपने हाथ आपको मारै । अपने कपड़े आपहि फारै ।।
मुहरे झाग मरोड़ै हाथा । कहै वहकेती फूहर बाता ।।
हाफै बहुत आपको गाली । जेंवत आवै पटकै थाली ।।
कबहुं शस्त्र सों मारन लागै । कबहूं कूँयें पड़ने भागै ।।
भली कहै तेहि भोग सुनावै । बुरे भले पर ईंट चलावै ।।
सबल देख शीला हो जावै । निबल देख बहु दुन्दि मचावै ।।
याका यतन करो मन भावै । चरणदास शुकदेव बतावै ।।

दोहा

जिहि घट आवै धूम सूं करै बहुतही खारि ।।
पति खोवै बुधि कूं हतै कहा पुरुष कहा नारि ।।१८२।।
वह बुद्धि भ्रष्ट करि डारै । वह मारहि मार पुकारै ।।
वह सब तन हिंसा छावै । कहिं दया न रहने पावै ।।
वह गुरु से बोलै बेंड़ा । साधों सूं डोलै ऐंड़ा ।।
वह हरि सों नेह छुटावै । वह नरक माहिं ले जावै ।।
वह आतमघाती जानौ । वह महा मूढ़ पहिचानौ ।।
सोंटौं की मार दिलावै । कबहूं कै शीश कटावै ।।
वह नीच कभी ना कहिये । ऐसे सूं डरता रहिये ।।
वह निकट न आवन दीजै । अरु क्षमा अंक भर लीजै ।।

जब क्षमा आय किया थाना । तब सबही क्रोध हिराना ।।
कहै गुरु शुकदेव खिलारी । सुनु चरणदास उपकारी ।।

दोहा

क्रोध अंग पूरो कियो कहूं मोह का अंग ।
जाहि लागै दुख दे घना कबहूं छोड़े संग ।।१८३।।
माया मोह बिछाइया जालसे भाल सँभारी ।।
आय आय तामें फँसे बहुत पुरुष बहु नारि।।७९।।
फँसे आय करि चाव सूं लै न गया नहिं कोय ।।
चरणदास यों कहत हैं पछिताये कह होय ।।८०।।
छूट सकै नहिं जाल सूं मिरगा ज्यों अकुलाय ।।
कूद कूद निकसो चहै ज्यों ज्यों उरझत जाय ।।८१।।
मोह शहत सम जानिये मक्खी सम जिय जान ।।
लालच लागे जित फँसे शीश धुनैं अज्ञान ।।८२।।
बन्दीखानो भवन है सब दिन धंधे जार ।।
मोह छुटावै राम सूं डारै नरक मँझार ।।८३।। १८८।।
लख चौरासी योनि में फिर वह भर में जाय ।।
ह्वाँसे निकसे कठिन सूं कबहूं औसर पाय ।।८४।। १८९।।

चौपई

तिरिया मोह महा बदलाई । मोह संतान सदा दुखदाई ।।
मोह कुटंब अरु भाई बंधा । समझे नहीं मूढ़ मति अंधा ।।
देव भूत जिहि कारण धावै । ठग चोरी करि खोट कमावै ।।
बस्ती भूषण बाहन मोहा । सब मिलि किया जीव सूं द्रोहा ।।
द्रब्य लाल अरु हीरा मोती । सब मिलि मोह लगावैं गोती ।।
मोह महल धरती अरु गाऊं । बड़ा मोह जो अपना नाऊं ।।
जामें फँसे रंक अरु राजा । तिहि कारण धंधा दुख साजा ।।
परकाजैं बहुतै दुख पाया । अपना सबही मूल गँवाया ।।
बड़े बड़े खेद उठाये सबहीं । भूले ध्यान राम का जबहीं ।।
जीते मोह शूरिमा कोई । मिलै राम कूं साधू सोई ।।
होय मुक्ति जग बहुरि न आवै । चरणदास शुकदेव बतावै ।।८५।। १९०।।

मोह निवारणके उपाय

दोहा

मोह बड़ा दुख रूप है ताकूं मार निकास ।।
प्रीति जगत की छोंड़ दे जब होवै निरबास ।।८६।। १९१।।
जग माहीं ऐसे रहो ज्यों जिह्वा मुखमाहिं ।।
घीव घना भक्षण करै तौ भी चिकनी नाहिं ।।८७।। १९२।।
जग माहीं ऐसै रहो ज्यों अम्बुज सर माहिं ।।
रहै नीर के आसरे पै जल छूवत नाहिं ।।८८।। १९३।।
ऐसा हो जो साध हो लिये रहै बैराग ।।
चरण कमल मों चित धरै जगमें रहै न पाग ।।८९।। १९४।।
मोह बली सब सूं अधिक महिमा कही न जाय ।।
जाको बांधो जग सबै छूटै ना बौराय ।।९०।। १९५।।

अथ लोभ अंग ।।

दोहा

लोभ नीच बर्णन करूं महापाप की खानि ।।
मंत्री जाका झूठ है बहुत अधर्मी जानि ।।९१।। १९६।।
तृष्णा जाकी जोय है सो अंधा करि देय ।।
घटी बढ़ी सूझै नहीं नहीं कालका भेय ।।९२।। १९७।।
दम्भ मकर छल भगल जो रहत लोभके संग ।।
मुये नरक लै जायँगे जीवत करै उदंग ।।९३।। १९८।।
देहैं धर्म छुटाय हो आन धर्म लेजाय ।।
हरि गुरु ते बेमुख करैं लालच लोभ लगाय ।।९४।। १९९।।
चहूं देश भरमत फिरै कलह कलपना साथ ।।
लोभ कंज उठ उठ लगैं दोउ पसारै हाथ ।।९५।। २००।।

चौपई

लोभी भक्त होय नहिं कबहीं । साधु पुराण कहत हैं सबहीं ।।
लोभी सती न होवै शूरा । लोभी दाता सन्त न पूरा ।।
लोभी हितू न होवै सांचा । लोभी रहै जगत में राचा ।।
लोभी रहै द्रव्य के माहीं । तन छूटै पै निकसै नाहीं ।।
लोभी करै जीव की घाता । लोभी करै कपट की बाता ।।

लोभी पाप न करता डरै । लोभी जाय कष्ट में परै ।।
लोभी बेंचै अपना सीसा । लोभी डूबै बिसवैबीसा ।।
गुरु शुकदैव बतावै हमकूं । सो वह कथा कहीं मैं तुमकूं ।।
चरणदास कहैं लोभ न कीजै । हरिके पद पंकज मन दीजै ।।९६।।

दोहा

चींटी बांदर खगन कूं लोभ बहुत दुखदीन ।।
याकूं तजि हरि कूं भजै चरणदास परबीन ।।९७।। २००।।
लोभ घटावै मान कूं करै जगत आधीन ।।
बोझ घटा भिष्टल करै करै बुद्धि को हीन ।।९८।। २०१।।
लोभ गये ते आवई महाबली संतोष ।।
त्याग सत्य कूं संगले कलह निवारण शोक ।।९९।।२०२।।
घट आवै सन्तोषही काह चहै जग भोग ।।
स्वर्ग आदिलौं सुखजिते सब कूं जानै रोग ।।१००।। २०३।।
संतोषी निरमल दिशा रहै राम लव लाय ।।
आसन ऊपर दृढ़ रहै इत उत कूं नहिं जाय ।।१०१।। २०४।।
काहू नहिं राखिये काहु बिधि को चाह ।।
परम संतोषी हुजिये रहिये बेपरवाह ।।१०२।। २०५।।
चाह जगत की दास है हरि अपना न करै ।।
चरणदास यों कहत हैं व्याधा नाहिं टरै ।।१०३।। २०६।।
अथ अभिमान अंग

दोहा

चार अंग पूरे किये कहूं गर्ब गुण गाय ।।
बहुत सिकंडी भारिया शिर पर छत्र फिराय ।।१०४।। २०७।।
अभिमानी चढ़िकरि गिरे गये बासना माहिं ।।
चौरासी भरमत भये क्योंहीं निकसै नाहिं ।।१०५।। २०८।।
अभिमानी मीजे गये लूट लिये धन बाम ।।
निर अभिमानी हो चले पहुँचे हरि के धाम ।।१०६।। २०९।।
चरणदास कहै आपा थपै गिनै आपको पाँच ।।
मान बड़ाई कारने सहै जगत की आंच ।।१०७।। २१०।।
करै बड़ाई कारने परपंची छल धूत ।।

अभिमानी फूले फिरैं ज्यों मर्कट का भूत ।।१०८।। २११।।
अभिमानी मुक्ति न होई । अभिमानी मति अपनी खोई ।।
ऐंठ अकड अभिमानी माहीं । अभिमानी नीचा हो नाहीं ।।
बिन नान्हापन सुख नहिं पावै । आनँद पद कूं कैसे जावै ।।
झूठ कपट अभिमानी खेले । कंचन बर्तन माटी मेले ।।
भगल दंभ नितही मन माहीं । निकट सांच कभी आवै नाहीं ।।
हूं हूं हूं करताही डोलै । काहूते सीधा नहिं बोलै ।।
इन लक्षण जीवत दुख पावै । नरक माहिं तन छूटै जावै ।।
चरणदास शुकदेव बतावै । पूरा सो अभिमान नशावै ।।१०९।।

दोहा
चरणदास यों कहत हैं सुनियो सन्त सुजान ।।
मुक्ति मूल आधीनता नरक मूल अभिमान ।।११०।। २१२।।
रूपवन्त होकर गरवावै । कोई मोसम दृष्टि न आवै ।।
तरुणापा पाकर गरवाना । वह अंधरा होवै राना ।।
कहै धन मधिमें परवीना । सब मेरेही हैं आधीना ।।
कहै कुल अभिमानी सूचा । मैं सब जातिन में हूं ऊंचा ।।
वह विद्या गर्व जु भारी । करै वाद विवाद अनारी ।।
अरु भूप करै अभिमाना । उन आपै ही कूं जाना ।।
उन काल नहीं पहिंचाना । सो मार करै घनसाना ।।
यम बाँधि पकरि लै जावैं । वै बहुतै त्रास दिखावैं ।।
गुरि शुकदेव चितावै । तोहिं परगट नैन दिखावैं ।।१११।।
जब कहा जाय अभिमाना । मेरा नीका सुन यह ताना ।।
फिर डारै नरक मँझारी । सुनि चेतो अरु नर नारी ।।
तौ मद मत्सरता तजि दीजै । साधों के ही चरण गहीजै ।।
हरि भक्ति करो चित लाई । जब सकल व्याधि छुठि जाई ।।
कर जाति वरण कुल दूरा । हो सतसंगति में पूरा ।।
जब मुक्त धाम कूं पावै । फिर गर्भ योनि नहिं आवै ।।
कहैं गुरु शुकदेव बखानौ । यह चरणदास मन आनौ ।।११२।।

दोहा
मन में लाय विचारि कूं दीजै गर्व निकार ।

नन्हापन जब जाय है छूटै सकल विकार ।।११३।। २१३।।
पांचौ उतरैं भूत जब ह्वैहो ब्रह्म अरूप ।
आनँद पद कूं पाय हौ जित है मुक्त स्वरूप ।।११४।। २३४।।
पांच प्रेत जो ये कहे सदगुरु के परताप ।
शील अंग अब कहत हूं जासूं छूटै पाप ।।११५।। २१६।।
इति पंचप्रेत वर्णन

१३ पंचप्रेत निवारण मन्त्र शील अंग वर्णन

दोहा

अब मैं गाउं शील कूं ये हो संत सुजान ।
नर नारी सबही सुनो दै दै चित बिधि कान ।।२१६।।
रूप गुणी कुलवंत जो अरु होवै धनवन्त ।
शील बिना शोभा नहीं विष्टै/भिष्टै नरक पडंत ।।२१७।।
शील बिना जो तप करै करै शील बिन दान ।
योग युक्ति करै शील बिन सो कहिये अज्ञान।।२१८।।
शील बड़ा ही योग है जो कर जानै कोय ।
शील विहीनौ चरणदास कबहुँ मुक्ति नहिं होय ।।२१९।।
सब शुभ लक्षण तो विषे शील न आया एक।
जप तप निष्फलजारिंगे चरणहिं दास विवेक।।२२०।।
पूजा संयम नेम जो यज्ञ करै चितलाय ।
चरणदास कहै शील बिन सभी अकारथ जाय ।।२२१।।
सोई सति सोई शूरमा सोइ दाता अधिकाय ।
शील लिये नितही रहै तौ निष्फल नहिं जाय।।२२२।।
शील अंग उंचो अधिक उवतीसौं के बीच ।
जा घट शील न आइया सो घट कहिये नीच ।।२२३।।
शील न उपजै खेत में शील न हाट बिकाय ।
जो हो पूरा टेक का लेवे अंग उपजाय ।।२२४।।
शील बिना नरकै परै शील विना यम दंड ।
शील विना भरमत फिरै सात द्वीप नव खंड ।।२२५।।
शील विना भटकत फिरै चौरासी के माहिं ।
पहिने होवै प्रेतही या में संशय नाहिं ।।२२६।।
सब तजि सो वो शील कूं राम नाम लौ लाय ।
जीवत शोभा जगत में मुये मुक्ति ह्वै जाय ।।२२७।।
जाको शील सुभाव है जाकी दूर बलाय ।

ताकी कीरति जगत में सुन हो कान लगाय ।।२२८।।
शील रहेते सब रहै जेते हैं शुभ अंग ।
ज्यों राजा के रहते रहै फौज को संग ।।२२९।।
सत्य गया तौ क्या रहा शील गया सब झाड ।
भक्ति खेत कैसे बचै टूट गई जब बाड ।।२३०।।
ज्वानी शील न राखिया बिगड गई सब देह ।
अब पछितावा क्या करै मुख पर उडिया खेह ।।२३१।।
शील गये शोभा घटै या दुनियाँ के माहिं ।
कूकर ज्यों झिड़क्यो फिरै कहिं भी आदर नाहिं ।।२३२।।
शील गये गुरु सूं फिरै हरि सों बेमुख होय ।
चरणदास कहँ लौं कहैं सर्वस डारै खोय ।।२३३।।
धीक जीवन संसार में जाको शील नशाय ।
जग में फिर फिर होत है मुये ताचना पाय ।।२३४।।
शील कसैला आँवला और बड़ों के बोल ।
पाछे देवैं स्वाद वे चरणदास कहि खोल ।।२३५।।
शील निरोगा नींब सा औगुण डारै खोय ।
पहिले करुवा दुख लगै पाछे गुण सुख होय ।।२३६।।
लाख यही उपदेश है एक शील कूं राख ।
जन्म सुधारो हरि मिलौ चरणदास की साख ।।२३७।।
शीलवंत चरण का जो चरणोदक लेय ।
रोग दोष मिटि जायँ सब रहै न यम का भेय ।।२३८।।
आठ अंग सूं शीलही जा घट माहिं होय ।
चरणदास यों कहत है दुर्लभ दर्शन सोय ।।२३९।।
शीलवंत दर्शन बड़े देखत पातक जाय ।
वचन सुनै मन शुद्ध हो खोटी दृष्टि सिराय ।।२४०।।
शील सरोवर न्हाई करि करौ राम की सेव ।
या सम तीरथ और ना कहिया गुरु शुकदेव ।।२४१।।
शील अंग पूरो कियो महिमा अधिक अपार ।
दया अंग वर्णन करूं समझै छूटै विकार ।।२४२।।

दया अंग वर्णन

दोहा

परमारथ में दया बड़ जो घट उपजै आय ।
परगत हो निर्वैता कर्म गाँठि खुल जाय ।।२४३।।
स्थावर जंगम चर अचर या जग में होय कोय ।
सबही पै हित राखिये सुख दानी ही होय ।।२४४।।
भोजन करौ सँभाल करि पानी पीजौ छान ।
हरा वृक्ष नहिं तोड़िये कर्म बचै यों जान ।।२४५।।
औरौ बहुत विचारि ले जामें लगै न कर्म ।
यही तपस्या जानिये यही दया यहि धर्म ।।२४६।।
इक इन्द्रीय दो इन्द्रियाँ ती इन्द्री अरु चार ।
पंच इन्द्री लौ जीव की हिंसा अकस निवार ।।२४७।।
खावै वस्तु विचारिकै बैठे ठौर विचार ।
जो कुछ करै विचारि करि किरिया यही अचार ।।२४८।।
मन सूं रहु निर्वैरता मुख सूं मीठा बोल ।
तन सूं रक्षा जीव की चरणदास कहि खोल ।।२४९।।
करुवा वचन न बोलिये तन सूं कष्ट न देहु ।
अपना सा जी जानिकै बनै तो दुख हरि लेहु ।।२५०।।
मुख सूं जो करुवा कहै तन सूं देवै कष्ट ।
यही जु हिंसा जानिये दया धर्म जा नष्ट ।।२५१।।
दश इन्द्री मन ग्यारवाँ करि विचार ले जान ।
इनहीं सूं सुख दीजिये चरणदास पहिंचान ।।२५२।।
काहू दुख नहिं दीजिये दुर्जन हो कै मीत ।
सुखदाई सब जगत को गहो दया की रीत ।।२५३।।
कोमलता पर पीरता सज्जनता निर्दोष ।
सभी दया के अंग हैं इनते पावै मोष ।।२५४।।
दया ज्ञान का मूल है दया भक्ति का जीव ।
चरणदास यों कहत है दया मिलावै पीव ।।२५५।।
दया नहीं तौ कुछ नहीं सबही थोथी बात ।
बाहर कथनी सोहनी भीतर लागी घात ।।२५६।।
छापै तिलक बनायके माला पहिरी दोय ।
दया बिना बग सम वही साधरूप नहिं होय ।।२५७।।
दया न आई घट विषे हीया बड़ा कठोर ।
यह नगरी कैसे बसै तामें हिंसा चोर ।।२५८।।

पंडिताई बहुतें करी दया न राखी जीव ।
छाँछि छाँछि तौ लेलई डारि दया तत घीव ।।२५९।।
तोहिं पण्डित मैं कह कहूँ मूरख कै परबीन ।
लिया न तैं मत सूप का चलनी का मत लीन ।।२६०।।
दया गहेते सब नशे पाप ताप दुख द्वन्द्व ।
ऐसी परम पुनीत कूं तजै सो मूरख अन्ध ।।२६१।।
दया विना नर पतित है दया विना नर दुष्ट ।
दया विना सुनते बने सबही थोथी गुष्ट ।।२६२।।
जन्म मरण छूटै नहीं नाहीं कर्म्म नशाहिं ।
दया बिन बदला भरै चौरासी के माहिं ।।२६३।।
काम क्रोध मोह लोभ से गर्व आदि भजि जाहिं ।
चरणदास कहैं दया जो घट में पहुँचे आहिं ।।२६४।।
जितने वैरी जीव के तिन में रहै न एक ।
चरणदास यों कहत है दया जो आवै नेक ।।२६५।।
दुख भाजैं सुख हों घनै काया नगरी ढंग ।
हिंसा रानी जो भजै लेकर अपनो संग ।।२६६।।
धन्य दया धनि शील कूं जिनसे रीझे राम ।
गुरु शुकदेव बतावई सबही सुधरैं काम ।।२६७।।
इति पंचप्रेतनिवारण मंत्र

१४ अथ मायारूप वर्णन

बैठा गुरु सूं चलता चेला। सुखी होय रहै रैन अकेला ॥
दया क्षमा रख राम सुहाती। बात कहैं करुवी नहिं ताती ॥
बिन जाचै उपदेश न दीजै। तरकी सूं चर्चा नहिं कीजै ॥
मौन गह थोरा सा बोलै। पलक न मिलैं नैन रहै खोले ॥
दृष्टि राख नासाके आगे। सत्य वचन मीठा मुख भाषे ॥
रसना उलट अकाश चढ़ावै। बिनहीं बादल जल बरसावै ॥
पवन साधि मल कूं ठहरावै। कामिनि कनकरुप बिसरावै ॥
आसन अडिग सुरत अनहद में। अन्तर खोल मिलै नहिं जग में ॥
चरणदास शुकदेव बतावै। ऐसा होय महन्त कहावै ॥

दोहा
जो बोलै तो हरि कथा मौन गहै तो ध्यान।
चरणदास यह धारण धारै सो सुज्ञान ॥२३८॥
माया की अस्तुति करूं होय रही संसार।
अद्भुत लीला कर रही शोभा अगम अपार ॥२६९॥
माया सकल पसार है नाना रँग बहु क्रान्ति।
जहँ लग यह आकारही चंचल मिथ्या भ्रांति ॥२७०॥
जैसे सुपना रैन का मुख दर्पण के माहिं।
भासै है पर है नहीं ज्यों तरुवर की छाहिं ॥२७१॥
यह माया सबही को मोहै। होय न वश अस को जग है ॥
यह तौ बहुत सोहनी लागै। सबही नर नारिन को पागै ॥
कहिं चमक दमक बहुरूपा। अरु कहीं रंक कहीं भूपा ॥
अरु जहँ तहँ बहुत तमासे। वह भाँति भाँतिही भासे ॥
अरु काम क्रोध मद लोभा। अरु मान बड़ाई शोभा ॥
अरु पाँचौं इन्द्री जानौ। सब माया रूप पिछानौ ॥
अरु पांच तत्त्व गुण तीनों। सो मायाही कूं चीनों ॥

वह मकर पेच छल जानै । अरु पहर पहर बहुवानै ।।
अरु शुकदेव जनावै । सब माया खेल दिखावै ।।

दोहा

जेते सुख संसार के सबही माया जार ।
तामें दो कण का धरै एक द्रव्य इक नार ।।२७२।।
लालच लागे चाव सूं गिरे आयकरि लोय ।
फँसे आप सूं आपही गहि नहिं लाया कोय ।।२७३।।
पाँचौ इन्द्री सों लखै सो माया आकार ।
याही सेती सब भयो जहँ लग है साकार ।।२७४।।
अरु माया रूप अनन्ता । कोई जानै साधू सन्ता ।।
कहा सुना अरु देखा । सब माया रूप विशेखा ।।
आठ सिद्धि नौ माया । जहँ योगी तपी भुलाया ।।
अरु माया फंदे माहीं । सब जीव आइ फँसि जाहीं ।।
वे नरक माहिं दुख पावैं । यम छप्पन त्रास दिखावैं ।।
फिर भुगतै लख चौरासी । वे गरभ योहि के वासी ।।
वे पशू देश धरि धावैं । नहिं मुक्ति ठिकाना पावैं ।।
चरणदास कहैं नर चेतौ । तजौ माया ही कूं हेतौ ।।

दोहा

जगत वासना के तजै माया की न बसाय ।
करम छुटै मिटि जीवता मुक्त रूप हो जाय ।।२७५।।

१५ इन्द्री वर्णन मन

दोहा

फँसे न इन्द्री स्वाद में चरण कमल में ध्यान।
पर आशा कोइ न रहै लगैं न माया बान ।।२७६।।
सबसे अधिकी ज्ञान है तासे उँचो ध्यान।
ध्यान मिलावे पीव कूं पावै पद निरवान ।।२७७।।
ध्याता ध्येय कैसे मिलै होंय न बिच में ध्यान।
तीनों एक हुये विना लहै न पद निरवान ।।२७८।।
इन्द्रिन के वश मन रहै मन के वस रहे बुद्धि।
कहौ ध्यान कैसे लगै ऐसा जहां विरुद्धि ।।२७९।।
जित जित इन्द्री जात हैं तित मन कूं लै जात।
बुधि भी संगहि जात है यह निश्चय कर बात ।।२८०।।
जित इन्द्री मन हूं गया रही कहा सूं बुद्धि।
चरणदास यों कहत हैं करि देखो तुम शुद्धि ।।२८१।।
इन्द्री मनके वश कहै मनकर बुधिके संग।
बुधि राखै हरि पद जहां लागै ध्यान अभंग ।।२८२।।
इन्द्री मन मिल होत है विषय वासना चाह।
उपजै जैसे कामही नारी मिल अरु नाह ।।२८३।।
न्यारे न्यारे तत रहैं होत न कछू उपाध।
जुदे राख मन इन्द्रियन गुरुगम साधन साध ।।२८४।।
इन्द्रिन सूं मन जुदा करि सुरत निरत करि शोध ।।
उपजै ना विष वासना चरणदास कर बोध ।।२८५।।
इन्द्री रोकेते रुके और यतन नहिं कोय।
मन चंचल रिझवार है रसक सवादी सोय ।।२८६।।
चलौ करै थिर ना रहै कोटि यतन करि राख।
यह जबहीं वश होयगा इन्द्रिन के रसनाख ।।२८७।।
न्यारे न्यारे चहत हैं अपने अपने स्वाद।

इन पांचों में प्रीति है कछ्रू न वाद विवाद ।।२८८।।
दुर्जन के फूटे बिना तेरी होय न जीत ।
चरणहि दास विचारि करि ऐसी कहिये रीत ।।२८९।।
जुदी जुदी पांचौ कहूँ एक एक का भेद ।
जो कोइ इन कूं वश करै सबही छूटै खेद ।।२९०।।
नेत्र इन्द्री यह इन्द्री आँख विचारो । सो देत महादुख भारो ।।
वह राग द्वेष उपजावै । अरु हरष शोक लै आवै ।।
सो रूप माहिं फँसि जावै । तन मन में व्याधि उठावै ।।
वह देह और के हाथा । करि डारै बहुत अनाथा ।।
वह फंदे माहीं डारै । अरु काम अगिनि में जारै ।।
यह डोलै दौरी दौरी । कर चित बिधि की गति औरी ।।
कोइ साधु शूरमा मौड़े । जग सेती नैना तोड़ै ।।
कहै चरणदास सुनि लीजै । कुछया का यतन करीजै ।।

दोहा
दीपक क्रिया निहारि करि गिरै पतंग ज्यों जाय ।
कछ्रू हाथ आवे नहीं उलटो आप जराय ।।२९१।।
उन तन मन सभी जराया । कछु भोंदू हाथ न आया ।।
अरु विषय वासना फैला । जब छुटा राम का गैला ।।
तौ मुक्ति कहां सों होई । दिया जन्म पदारथ खोई ।।
अब क्या शिर मारै कोई । घरही में दुर्जन सोई ।।
यह दृष्टि सदा की वैरी । जो सूरत बिगारै तेरी ।।
वह माया मोह लगावै । अरु चौरासी भरमावै ।।
शरम सकुच सब खोवै । अरु बीज कुबुधि का बोवै ।।
यह ठग चोरी की बानी । अरु जार करम अगवानी ।।
यह पानय सभी घटावै । यम पुर के त्रास दिखावै ।।
कहै गुरु शुकदेवा । ये आँख महादुख देवा ।।

दोहा
ऐसी इन्द्री आँख की सो अपना नहिं होय ।
गुरु शुकदेव बतावई चरणदास सुन लोय ।।२९२।।

दर्शन कीजै साधुका कौ गुरु का कर लोय ।।
जहँ तहँ ब्रह्महिं देखिये दुबिधा दुर्मति खोय ।।२९३।।
वैरी मिंतर एकसा एकै रूप कुरूप ।
ऐसी होवै दृष्टिही जब समझै मन भूप ।।२९४।।
श्रवण इन्द्री २ सुन दूजै इन्द्री काना । सो गुरु परतापै जाना ।।
जब सुनै कामरस रीता । तब भूलै पढ़ सुन गीता ।।
मन उपजै काम तरंगा । तब होत ध्यान में भंगा ।।
फिरि लोभ वचन सुन औरै । तब तृष्णा चहुँ दिशि दौरै ।।
कहिं द्रव्य हाथ लगि जावै । यों शोचि शोचि दुख पावै ।।
कहैं ठग चोरीकर लाऊं । कहिं गडा दबा हो पाऊं ।।
काहू सुनै जु दौलत बंधा । मनहीं मन में रोवै अंधा ।।
यों उपजै अधिकी लोभा । जब बढ़ै पाप की गोभा ।।
कहैं चरणहिंदास विचारी । सुन चेतो नर अरु नारी ।।
फिर सुनैं बड़ाई कुल की । जब पुलक हँसत है मुल की ।।
जो अपनी सुनै बड़ाई । जब अहूं होत अकड़ाई ।।
फिर करन बड़ाई लागै । सोता ज्यों कूकर जागै ।।
जब उपजै बहु अभिमाना । अरु नेक न होवै नान्हा ।।
परनिन्दा बहुत सुहावै । नहिं और बड़ाई भावै ।।
अहंकार बड़ा मन माहीं । आधीन बिना गति नाहीं ।।
सुनि उपजै तामस अंगा । जब करै बहुत ही दंगा ।।
मन क्रोध रूप हो जावै । उठ उठकर मारन धावै ।।
कभी सुनै मोह के बैना । लगै हर्ष शोक दुख दैना ।।
जब सुन कुटुँब की नीकी । तब करि खुशी बहु जी की ।।
कोइ कुटुँब माहिं दुख पावै । सुन रो रो नैन गवावै ।।
जो हिरन कान वश हूवा । तौ तीर लगा करि मूवा ।।
शुकदेव कहैं सुन जानौ । सब कान विकार पिछानौ ।।

श्रवण का सत्कर्म

दोहा

मन दे सुनिये हरि कथा ।।
सुनिये हरि यश कान । ताहि विचार जु कीजिये होय भक्ति का ज्ञान ।।२९५।।
उपजै ज्ञान भक्ति अरु योगा । सुनि सुनि उपजै राम वियोगा ।।

उपजै प्रेम अनन्या उमाहा । होय उछाह दरश का चाहा ।।
सुनि सुनि उपजै लक्षण साधू । सुनि सुनि पावै भेद अगाधू ।।
उपजै साधू संत की सेवा । गुरुमुख होय सुनै नहिं भेवा ।।
सुनि सुनि उपजै भय अरु लाजा । सोवै सकल सँवारन काजा ।।
सुनि सुनि यती सती हो जावै । नान्हा हो अभिमान नशावै ।।
सुनि सुनि छूटै यम की त्रासा । चौरासी में लहै न बासा ।।
सुनि सुनि चार पदारथ पावै । आवागमन के बीज जरावै ।।
सुनि सुनि काग हंस हो जाई । चरणदास शुकदेव बताई ।।

दोहा
सुनि सुनि उपजै सुबुधि ही लागै हरि का रंग ।
सुनि सुनि उपजै कुबुधि ही खोटी उठै तरंग ।।२९६।।
ऐसी इन्द्री कान की जाके मुगल सुभाव ।
कथा कीरतन हीं सुनौ करि करि कोटि उपाव ।।२९७।।
वचन सुनो गुरु साधु के मन कूं लावो मोर ।
विषय वासना सूं निकसे आवै हरि की ओर ।।२९८।।

जिह्वा इंद्री ३
दोहा
सरवन इन्द्री मैं कही दोनों अंग दिखाय ।
जिह्वा इन्द्री कहत हैं चरणदास चित लाय ।।२९९।।
कुटिल जु इन्द्री जीभ की चाहै षटरस स्वाद ।
या वश हो औगुण करै जन्म जाय बरबाद ।।३००।।
यह बहुत चटोरी कहिये । याही तें डरते रहिये ।।
यह चोरी भी करवावै । यह पकड़ बन्ध में ध्यावै ।।
करै याहि कारण जारी । यह करे बहुत ही ख्वारी ।।
यह अमल खान सिखलावै । अरु गाली मार दिलावै ।।
अरु बहुतै झूठ बुलावै । हो मीत नरक ले जावै ।।
खेले याही कारण जूवां । दुनियाँ में फिट फिट हूवां ।।
ये पांचौ ऐब सुनाउं । रसना में सभी दिखाऊं ।।
यह महा अपरबल जानौ । अरु रणजीता हो भानौ ।।

दोहा

जिह्वा के जीते बिना गये जन्म सब हार।
चरणदास यों कहत हैं भये जगत में ख्वार ।।३०१।।
बंशी डारी ताल में मछरी लागी आय।
जिह्वा कारण जिव दियो तलफि तलफि मरि जाय ।।३०२।।
तजा न जिह्वा स्वाद कूं वा सँग दीन्हें प्रान।
जो कोइ ऐसा जगत में सो अज्ञानी जान ।।३०३।।
यासूं ले हर नामहीं गुण वादही भाख।
जो बोलै तौ सांचही नाहीं मुख में राख ।।३०४।।
मीठा वचन उचारियो नवता सब सूं बोल।
हिरदै माहिं विचारि करि जब मुख बाहर खोल ।।३०५।।
बिना स्वादही खाइये राम भजन के हेत।
चरणदास कहै शूरमा ऐसे जीतो खेत ।।३०६।।
जिन जीता है जीभ कूं तिन जीती सब देह।
कहै गुरु शुकदेव जी मुक्ति धाम फल लेह ।।३०७।।
रसना जीतै भक्त जो सो योगी सो साध।
अगम पन्थ वहि पग धरै पहुँचै देश अगाध ।।३०८।।

त्वचा इन्द्री ४

त्वचा सु इन्द्री काम की नितही खेलै दाव।
पशु पक्षी असुरा नरा फँसे आयकरि चाव ।।३०९।।
यह त्वचा सुमल मल मांजै। अरु काजल सुरमा आंजै ।।
यह तेल फुलेल लगावै। अरु चिकना गात बनावै ।।
अरु वस्तर भूषण पहिरे। कहै अंजन मंजन गहिरे ।।
अरु सपरस की विधि ठानै। सब याही कूं सुख मानै ।।
अरु फँसे आयकरि दोऊ। अब निकसन कैसे होऊ ।।
हित गांठ पेंच गहि दीन्हा। दोउ नेह वचन बहु कीन्हा ।।
अरु एक एक नै बाधा। वह समझै नाहीं आधा ।।
अब शीश धुनैं पछितावैं। दोउ चले नरक कूं जावैं ।।
कहै चरणदास नहिं जानौ। तुम औगुण ना पहिंचानौ ।।

दोहा

त्वचा स्वाद सब वश भये फँदे जगत के माहिं ।
जो कोई निकसौ चहै सो भी निकसै नाहिं ।।३१०।।
धोखे की हथिनी लखी आयो गज ललचाय ।
खंदक माहीं रुकि गयो शीश धुनै पछिताय ।।३११।।
कछू हाथ आयो नहीं परो फन्द में जाय ।
मैन महावत वश भयो शिर में अंकुश खाय ।।३१२।।
जंगल में आनन्द सूं बहुतै केलि कराय ।
अब तौ द्वारे सूत के परो बन्ध में आय ।।३१३।।
ऐसेही यह नर फँसो देखि कामिनी रूप ।
जन्म गँवायो दुख भरो पड़ो अविद्या कूप ।।३१४।।
करी न हरि की भक्तिही गुरुसेवा तजि दीन ।
सुनी न हरि की गुण कथा सतसंगत नहिं कीन ।।३१५।।
फिर ऐसो कब होयगो पावै मानुष देह ।
अब तौ चौरासी विषे जाय कियो उन गेह ।।३१६।।
जीतौ इन्द्री त्वचा की कहिया श्रीशुकदेव ।
यासे तपही कीजिये चरणदास सुन लेव ।।३१७।।
शीत उष्ण का दुख नहिं मानै । कोमल सकत एक करि जानै ।।
तपसूं काया उमर गवाँवै । अष्ट सुगन्ध निकट नहिं जावै ।।
आन त्वचा स्पर्श नहिं करै । काम अगिनि हिय में ना जरै ।।
काया ताबन करनी ठानै । यही तपस्या मन में आनै ।।
त्वचा सु इन्द्री जीतो ऐसे । मैं यह भेद बतायो जैसे ।।
गुरु शुकदेव बतावै सबही । चरणदास कर तन सूं तपही ।।

दोहा

त्वचा सुइन्द्री वश किये छूटै काम कलेश ।
यत शत शील सन्तोष सूं लगै न माया लेश ।।३१८।।
नासिका इन्द्री ५

दोहा

त्वचा अंग पूरो कियो कहूं नासिका अंग ।

ता बस अलिसुत जी दियो जाको कहूं प्रसंग ।।३१९।।
वास आस गुंजत फिरौ बैठौ कमल मँझार ।
सूर छिपे से मुँदि दयो अब शिर दै दै मार ।।३२०।।
कुँजर आयो ताल पै जल पीवन के काज ।
प्यास बुझी करने लगो खेल करन को साज ।।३२१।।
खेल करत कमल ही गह्यो लीन्हो ताहि उपारि ।
फेरि दियो मुख माहिं हीं चाबि गयो दे जाड़ ।।३२२।।
ऐसै ही ये नर फँसे परे काल मुख जाय ।
चरणदास यों कहत हैं चलै जन्म गवाँय ।।३२३।।
सुगँध ओर हरषै नहीं दुरगन्धै न रिसाय ।
ऐसी जीतै नासिका मन भँवरा ठहराय ।।३२४।।
समझन कूं तुक एक है भूलन कूं तुक लाख ।
गुण औगुण इन्द्री कहे सो तू मन में राख ।।३२५।।
जो इन्द्रिन के वश भयो बाँधो नरकै जाय ।
चौरासी भरमत फिरै गर्भ योनि दुख पाय ।।३२६।।
जो इन्द्रिन के वश भयो पावै ना आनन्द ।
बार बार जग माहहीं छूटै ना सम्बन्ध ।।३२७।।
भक्ति माहिं चित ना लगै सबही बिगड़ै काम ।
जो इन्द्री के वश भयो ताको मिलै न राम ।।३२८।।
चरणदास यों कहत है इन्द्री जीतन ठान ।
जग भूलै हरि कूं मिलै पावै पद निर्वान ।।३२९।।
इन्द्री जीतै सो ब्रह्मज्ञानी । इन्द्री जीतै सोई ध्यानी ।।
इन्द्री जीतै सो हरिदासा । अमर लोक में पावै वासा ।।
इन्द्री जीतै सोई सिद्धा । अष्टकला अरु पावै ऋद्धा ।।
इन्द्री जीतै सोई शूरा । इन्द्री जीतै सोई जन पूरा ।।
इन्द्री जीतै सो सतवन्ता । इन्द्री जीतै गुणी महन्ता ।।
इन्द्री जीतै राम रिझावे । इन्द्री जीतै सब कुछ पावै ।।
इन्द्री जीतै सो संन्यासी । इन्द्री जीतै सोई उदासी ।।
इन्द्री जीतै सब फलदायक । इन्द्री जीतै सब कुछ लायक ।।
इन्द्री जीतै छुटै विदेशा । यो जग में कछु लगै न लेशा ।।
इन्द्री जीतै परम सुखारा । निश्चय पहुँचे हरि दरबारा ।।
इन्द्री जीतै सो रणजीता । इन्द्री जीतै आतम मीता ।।

इन्द्री जीतै ध्यान लगावै । सो निश्चय ईश्वर ह्वै जावै ।।
इन्द्री जीतै मिलै भगवंता । इन्द्री जीतै जीवनमुक्ता ।।
चरणदास सुन कहैं शुकदेवा । इन्द्री जीतै सो गुरुदेवा ।।
मनका कार्य

दोहा

मन इन्द्रिन के वश भयो होय रह्यो बेढंग ।
आपा बिसरो जग रलो हुवो जो नाना रंग ।।३३०।।
आवै तरंग क्रोध की होत युवा को रूप ।
काम लहर कबहूं उठै ताके होत स्वरूप ।।३३१।।
लोभ कामना जब उठै जभी लोभ रँग होय ।
मोह कल्पना के उठै मोह वरण हो सोय ।।३३२।।
मनहीं खेलै खेल सब मनहीं कर अभिमान ।
मनहीं यह जग ह्वै रहो अब सुनु मनका ज्ञान ।।३३३।।
कबहूं यह मन होवै गिरही । कबहूं यह मन होवै विरही ।।
कबहूं यह मन होवै रोगी । कबहूं यह मन होवै शोगी ।।
कबहूं यह मन होवै नारी । कबहूं यह मन राखै ख्वारी ।।
कबहूं यह मन दोरा डोलै । कबहूं यह मन टेढा बोलै ।।
कबहूं यह मन कुलका ऊंचा । कबहूं यह मन नकटा बूंचा ।।
कबहूं यह मन दुन्दि मचावै । कबहूं क्षमा शील घर आवै ।।
कबहूं यह मन होवै दाता । कबहूं करै सूमसी बाता ।।
चरणदास कहैं मन कूं जानौ । ऐसी विधि मन कूं पहिंचानौ ।।

दोहा

बहुरूपी बहुरंग या बहुत रंग बहु चाव ।
बहुत भांति संसार में करि करि घने उपाव ।।३३४।।
यह मन राजा होवै भोगी । यह मन त्यागी होवै योगी ।।
यह मन होवै हरि का भक्ता । यह मन होवै योग रु युक्ता ।।
यह मन होय विवेकी ज्ञानी । यह मन तपिया जपिया ध्यानी ।।
यह मन करै दया की बातैं । यह मन करै जीव की घातैं ।।
यह मन यती सती अरु शूरा । यह मन काशी पण्डित पूरा ।।

यह मन तीरथ वरत उपासी । यह मन ठकुरानी अरु दासी ।।
यह मन होवै देवी देवा । या मनका कोइ लहे न भेवा ।।
यह मन प्रेमी नेमी जनहीं । चरणदास कहै सब कुछ मनहीं ।।

दोहा
या मन के जाने बिना होय न कबहूं साध ।
जगत वासना ना छुटै लहै न भेद अगाध ।।३३५।।
तैं मन कूं जाना नहीं करी न याकी सार ।
चौरासी छूटै नहीं उपजा वारंवार ।।३३६।।
मन जीतना के उपाय मन कूं सत्संगति लै जावौ । कानो हरि यश कथा सुनावो ।।
भाँति भाँति के रंग ललचावै । तौ हरि के रँग क्यों न रँगावै ।।
तौ याको ज्ञानी ही कीजै । जक्त और जाने नहिं दीजै ।।
कै कीजै हरि ही का ध्यानूं । राम भक्ति में याकूं सानूं ।।
कै कीजै यह योगी पूरा । याहि सुनावो अनहद तूरा ।।
या मन कूं कीजै वैरागी । याकूं कीजै सर्वस त्यागी ।।
जग रँग उतरि ब्रह्म रँग लागै । जाते कर्म भर्म भय भागै ।।
चरणदास शुकदेव बतावै । मन फेरिन की राह दिखावै ।।

दोहा
मनने आयु गवाँइया ज्ञान बुझाया दीव ।
करम लगा भरमत फिरो मिलो न अपना पीव ।।३३७।।
दौरि दौरि रस ओरही होय रहा कंगाल ।
नातरु आगे भुप था ऊंचा बड़ा दयाल ।।३३८।।
पाँचौ इन्द्री स्वाद में भयो निपट आधीन ।
राज बड़ाई सब नशी भयो मूढ मति हीन ।।३३९।।
सरकी जाय विष ओरही बहुरि न आवै हाथ ।
भजन माहिं ठहरे नहीं जो गहि राखू बाथ ।।३४०।।
मन निश्चल आवै नहीं निकसि निकसि भजि जाय ।
चरणदास यों कहत हैं काहू की न बसाय ।।३४१।।
पचि हारे ज्ञानी तपी रहे बहुत शिर नाय ।
मन परेत सूं डर लगै ले डूबै मझधार ।।३४२।।

यह मन भूत समान है दौड़ै दांत पसार ।
बाँस गाड़ि उतरै चढ़ै सब बल जावै हार ।।३४३।।
ज्यों आतम में मन धरै हौय जहों लौ लीन ।
ठहरि रहै फिरि ना चलै सकल विकल हो क्षीन ।।३४४।।
भजै तौ जानि न दीजिये घेरि घेरि करि लाव ।
यह मन कूं परचाय करि ध्यानहिं माहिं लगाव ।।३४५।।
और कहौं विधि दूसरी सुनियो चित लगाय ।
राम नाम मन सूं जपै चंचलता थकि जाय ।।३४६।।
पवन रुकै जब मन थकै और दृष्टि ठहराय ।
ऐसी साधन साधिये गुरुगम भेद मिलाय ।।३४७।।
इन्द्री रोके मन रुके अरु उत्तम विधि एहु ।
चरणदास यों कहत हैं यह साधन करि लेहु ।।३४८।।
इन्द्रिन कूं मन वश करै मन कूं वश करै पौन ।
अनहद वशकर वाय कूं अनहद कूं लै तौन ।।३४९।।
याको नाम समाधि है मन तामें ठहराय ।
जन्म जन्म की वासना ताकूं दग्ध कराय ।।३५०।।
इन्द्री लपटै मन विषे मन लपटै बुधि माहिं ।
बुधि लपटै हरि ध्यान में फेरि होय लै जाहिं ।।३५१।।
दग्ध वासना होय जब आवागमन नशाय ।
कहै गुरु शुकदेवजी मुक्त रूप ह्वै जाय ।।३५२।।

१६ असत्य का वर्णन

मन के सगरे भेदही जाको दियो जिताव।
चरणदास यों कहत हैं झूठ सांच को न्याव ॥३६३॥
जो कोइ बोलै झूठही ताकूं लागै पाप।
जन्म जन्म छूटै नहीं दुख दे तीनों ताप ॥३६४॥
बोलै झूठ महा अपराधी। धर्म छुटै उठि लागै व्याधी ॥
झूठा सौ सौ सौगँध खाय। झूठा लेवे कर्म लगाय ॥
झूठा करै बिराना बुरा। झूठा लेवें जगत में गिरा ॥
झूठे की परतीत न होई। झूठा बोल न बोलै कोई ॥
झूठा हरि की भक्ति न पावै। झूठा घोर कुण्ड में जावै ॥
झूठे कूं लागै यम मार। झूठा चौरासी में ख्वार ॥
झूठ वचन का भारी दोष। झूठ की होय गती न मोष ॥
झूठे के नाहिं गुरू न राम। झूठे कूं नाहीं विश्राम ॥
चरणदास शुकदेव बतावैं। झूठें सबी नरक कूं जावैं ॥

दोहा
झूठे के मुँह दीजिये नोसादर का बाप।
डरा करै सकुचा रहै वह शरमिंदा आप ॥३५५॥
झूठे कूं हत्यारा जानौ। झूठे को ठग चोर पिठानौ ॥
झूठा कुटिल शराबी होय। झूठा कहिये कामी सोय ॥
झूठही को जानौ ज्वारी। समझि देखि सबही नर नारी ॥
सकल ऐब झूठे में पाऊं। एक एक क्या खोल दिखाऊं ॥
पांचौ खोट सबन के राजा। सो मैं कहे चितावन काजा ॥
झूठ पाप की कहिये खानी। सो वह करै पुण्य की हानी ॥
सबही अवगुण झूठे माहीं। चरणदास शुकदेव बताहीं ॥१०५॥

१७ सत्य वर्णन

दोहा

साँच बिना साधू नहीं कबहुँ न मिलि हैं राम ।
साँच विना गति ना लहै पावै ना निज धाम ।।१०६।।३५६।।
सत सत मुख सूं बोलोया सत ही चलिये चाल ।
सतही मन में राखिये सत ही रहिये नाल ।।१०७।।३५७।।
साँचे कूं ग्रह ना लगै सांचे कूं नहिं दाग ।
सांचे शाप न लागई सब दुख जावै भाग ।।१०८।।३५८।।
बड़ी तपस्या सांच है बड़ा बरत है सांच ।
जासों पाप सभी जरैं लगे न गर्भ की आंच ।।१०९।।३५९।।
जाका वचन मुड़ै नहीं सांचे सब व्यवहार ।
चरणदास त्रयलोक में कभी न आवै हार ।।११०।।३६०।।
सांचे के मनहीं में राम । सांचा करै न छल के काम ।।
सांचा होकर सुमिरण करै । आप तरै औरन लै तरै ।।
सतवादी की पति है सांच । ताकूं लगै न दिवकी आंच ।।
सांचे चोर चुराया घोड़ा । परमेश्वर ताका रँग मोड़ा ।।
और चोर चोरी सूं गया । सांच प्रताप अचम्भा भया ।।
और सांच प्रताप अनंता । सबही जानै साधू संता ।।
लाख बातका एकहि जोड़ । सांचा पुरुष सबन शिरमोड़ ।।
आवै सांच परम सुख पावै । चरणदास शुकदेव सुनावै ।।१११।।

दोहा

सांचे की पदवी बड़ी दुष्ट साध के माहिं ।
दोनों अस्तुतिही करैं निन्दक कोई नाहिं ।।११२।।३६१।।

१८ गुरुमुख वर्णन

दोहा

गुरू कहै सो कीजिये कर सो कीजै नाहिं ।
चरणदास की सीख सुन यही राख मन माहिं ।।११३।।३६२।।
कथा सुनी ब्रत हूं किये तीरथ किये अघाय ।
गुरुमुख के होये बिना जपतप निष्फल जाय ।।११४।।३६३।।

गुरुमुख लक्षण

अब गुरुमुख के लक्षण गांऊ । जुदे जुदे करि सब समझाऊं ।।
इनकूं समझ धरे हिय कोई । पूरा गुरुमुख कहिये सोई ।।
प्रथमहिं गुरु सों झूंठ न बोले । खोटी खरी करै सब खोले ।।
दूजे गुरु को पयन लगावै । निश्चय गुरु के चरण मनावै ।।
तीजे आज्ञाकारी जानौ । इन लक्षण गुरुमुखी पिछानौ ।।
जो कोइ गुरु का लेवै नाम । ताको निहुरि करै परणाम ।।
जो कहुं देखै गुरु का बाना । ताकूं जानै गुरू समाना ।।
चरणदास शुकदेव बखानै । गुरुभाई कूं गुरु सम जानै ।।

दोहा

गुरुभाई कूं पूजिये धरिये चनणन शीश ।
चरणोदक फिरि लीजिये गुरुमत विश्वाबीश ।।११६।।३६४।।
जो कहुँ गुरुका बस्तर पावै । हिये लगाय चूक दृग क्ष्यावै ।।
गुरूदेश का मानुष जावै । दै परिकर्मा बलि बलि जावै ।।
कहां दया करि दर्शन दीन्हें । मेरे पाप भये सब क्षीन्हें ।।
जो अपने गुरु द्वारे जइये । देखत पौरि बहुत हरषइये ।।
ह्वांई सूं दण्डवत जु कीजै । दर्शन करि करि सर्वस दीजै ।।

फिर ठाढो रहै जोरे हाथा। बैठे तब आज्ञा दे नाथा॥
जो बोले सो मन में धरिये। अपने अवगुण सबही हरिये॥
चरणदास शुकदेव बतावै। ऐसा गुरुमुख राम रिझावै॥११७॥

१९ साधू माहात्म्य

साधुन की निंदा बुरी मत कोइ कीजो भूल ।
दुनिया में दुख पाइ है रहे नरक में झूल ।।११८।। ३६५।।
साधु का निन्दक तन मन दुखी । साधु का निन्दक हो ना सुखी ।।
निन्दक साधु दरिद्री होय । निन्दक डारै सर्वस खोय ।।
साधु का निन्दक नरक मँझार । निश्चय खावै यम की मार ।।
साधु का निन्दक पूरा पापी । साधु का निन्दक डूबै आपी ।।
मूरख होय सो निन्दा करै । साधु संत कूं अवगुण धरै ।।
साधु का निन्दक श्वान समान । साधु का निंदक शूकी जान ।।
साधु राम की कहिये देह । निंदक के मुख माहीं खेह ।।
चरणदास निन्दा तजि दिजै । भक्तन की अस्तुति कीजै ।।

दोहा
साधुन की अस्तुति किये हरि अस्तुति होय ।
भक्तन की निन्दा किये प्रभु की निन्दा सोय ।।१२०।।३६६।।

२० अथ मोह छुड़ावन अंग वर्णन

कुणडलिया

भक्ति दृढ़ावन कूं कहै नाना ही परसंग ।
शुकदेव कृपा सों अब कहूं मोह छुटावन अंग ।।
मोह छुटावन अंग कोई हिय माहीं धारै ।
कुटुँब जानि सूं छूटि हरि चरणौ लागै ।।
चरणदास यों कहत है उपजे मन वैराग ।
जगत नींद हीं सूं खुलै चौथे पन में जाग ।।१२१।।

दोहा

गुरु पूजि जग छोड़िये भवसागर के द्वन्द्व ।
साधुन की संगति करौ तजौ जाति कुल बंद ।।१२२।। ३६७।।
बन्धु नारि सुत कुटुँब सब यम की फाँसी जान ।
तोहिं छुटावै राम सूं इन का कहा न मान ।।१२३।। ३६८।।
खैंचि पकड़ि ह्वां राखि है जहां मोह का जाल ।
जीवत दुख बहु भांति के मुये नरक ततकाल ।।१२४।। ३६९।।
या प्राणी कूं ठग लगै सकल कुटुँब परिवार ।
तिनमें दो बलवन्त हैं एक द्रव्य इक नारि ।।१२५।। ३७०।।
नारि किये दुख बहुत हैं बन्धन बधै अनेक ।
जो सुख चाहै जीव का तिरियो कूं मत पेख ।।१२६।। ३७१।।
द्रव्य माहिं दुख तीनि हैं यह तो निश्चय जान ।
आवत दुख राखत दुखी जात प्राण की हान ।।१२७।। ३७२।।
ताते इनकी प्रीति मन उठै तभी निरवार ।
ये दुर्जन दुखरूप हैं ऐसो करो विचार ।।१२८।। ३७३।।
जो कोई इनमें पगै तिनसों छूठै राम ।
चरणदास यों कहत हैं क्यों पावै हरिधाम ।।१२९।। ३७४।।
हेरि फेरि धन को करत बितै पहर इक रात ।

तीन पहर निशि के रहैं खोवै नारी साथ ।।१३०।। ३७५।।
नारि के फैलाव को दीखै न छोर ।
द्रव्य माहिं तृष्णा रहै चाहै लाख करोर ।।१३१।। ३७६।।
द्रव्य जोरि मरि जाय जब हो बैठे तहँ नाग ।
नारी में जो चित रहै ह्वै है कूकर काग ।।१३२।। ३७७।।
ऐसे ही भरमत फिरै लख चौरासी देह ।
कनक कामिनी कूं तजै जबलग नाहीं नेह ।।१३३।। ३७८।।
मूरख त्याग न करि सकै ज्ञानवंत तजि देह ।
चौंकायल मृग ज्यों रहै कहीं न साजै गेह ।।१३४।। ३७९।।
जो कोइ छोड़ै कुटुँब कूं ऐसी कर पहिंचान ।
जैसे छूटै बन्ध सूं यम जोरा सूं जान ।।१३५।। ३८०।।
जीवत यम तौ कुटुँब है घेरी घेरि दुख देय ।
ऐसे मानुष देह कूं लूटै ही तिन लेय ।।१३६।। ३८१।।
कै ठग सब कूं जानिये कै धारी कै चोर ।
रणजित कहै तू देख ले लूटत हैं निशि भोर ।।१३७।। ३८२।।
बाहर कलकल करत हैं भीतर लावहिं लाव ।
ऐसो बांधौ खैंचकरि छुटै हाथ नहिं पाव ।।१३८।। ३८३।।
जाल तौंक गलमें पड़ा ममता बेरी पांय ।
रसरी मूरख नेह की लीन्हें हाथ बंधाय ।।१३९।।३८४।।
डारि दियो अज्ञान में परो परो बिललाय ।
निकसन कूं जबहीं चहै कुतका मोह लगाय ।।१४०।।३८५।।
रखवारे जहँ पाँच हैं इन्द्रिन के रस जान ।
तबहि देह मुलाय कै जो कुछ उपजै ज्ञान ।।१४१।। ३८६।।
कुटुँब और इन पांच कूं एक मतो ही जान ।
प्राणी कूं जग में फँसा चहै खान अरु पान ।।१४२।। ३८७।।
ये सब स्वारथी ही लगैं इनका सगा न कोय ।
जो शिर मारै धरणि पर कल्प कल्प करि रोय ।।१४३।। ३८८।।
मात पिता सुत नारि की इन की उलटी रीति ।
जग में देह फँसाय कै करिकै प्रीतिहि प्रीति ।।१४४।। ३८९।।
जैसे वधिक बिछायकै जाल माहिं कण्डार ।
प्रीति करै पक्षी गहै पाछे करै जु ख्वार ।।१४५।। ३९०।।
जैसे ठग बहु प्यार करि भोलापनही देह ।

पहिले लड्डू खवायकै पाछे सरवस लेह ॥१४६॥ ३९१॥
हित सूं हरिण बोलायकै गोली मारै तान ।
चरणदास यों कहत है ऐसे इनकूं जान ॥१४७॥ ३९२॥
जल में वंशी डारिया अटकाया जहँ मास ।
मछरी जानै हित कियो लखो न अपनो नाश ॥१४८॥ ३९३॥
भोंदू यह गति ना लखी पड़ो कुमति के धंध ।
ज्यों की त्यों सूझी नहीं किया मोहने अंध ॥१४९॥ ३९४॥
सब ठग यह देखी नहीं कपट हेत नहिं जान ।
इनहीं में मिलकी चलौ समझौ ना अज्ञान ॥१५०॥ ३९५॥
अब इनके छल कहत हूं समझे होय उदास ।
जान ना ह्वांई रहै कहै चरणही दास ॥१५१॥ ३९६॥
अब इनके छल कहि समझाऊं । भिन्न भिन्न परगट दिखलाऊं ॥
पिता कहै तुम पुत्र हमारे । बहुत भरोसे मोहिं तुम्हारे ॥
अब तुम ऐसी विद्या पढ़ो । अपने कुल में ऊंचे चढ़ो ॥
सत संगति में कभी न जइये । अपने घर में चित्त लगइये ॥
हम तो हैं दुनिया के कूते । जाति वर्ण में होहिं सपूते ॥
कृत्य करो पालौ सुत वामा । कथा कीरतन कूं क्या कामा ॥
अब तुम ठौर हमारी हूजै । हमने किये सो तुमहू कीजै ॥
ऐसी बुद्धि बडाई दीन्ही । इनहू हिरदै में धरि लीन्ही ॥
चरणदास कहैं देखो प्यारा । मुये नरक जीवतही ख्वारा ॥

दोहा

देई ऐसी बुद्धि पिता, रहिये कुटुंब मँझारि ।
जो कुछ है सो जगत में, धन सम्पति सुत नारि ॥३९७॥
हरि की राह भुलाय करि, दीनहो कुटुंब चिताय ।
ताते दुख जग में घने, चौरासी भरमाय ॥३९८॥
अब सुन माता हू की बातैं । अपना जानि खियावै तातैं ॥
द्रव्य काज उद्यमहीं कीजै । लै माता की गोदी दीजै ॥
करै कमाई सोइ सपूता । नाहीं तौ वह पूत कपूता ॥
नारी कूं भूषण पहिरावो । सुत पुत्री को व्याह रचायो ॥
पूजो पित्तर देवी देवा । सकसल कुटुंब की कीजै सेवा ॥

अपने कुलको न्योति जिमावो । ताते बहुत बडाई पावो ।।
बहु विधि स्वारथ ही सिखलावै । परमारथ की राह भुलावै ।।
बार बार जग में उरझावै । ऐसे तौ नितही चलि आवै ।।
जितका तित ह्वांई रखि लीन्हा । चरणदास कहैं जान न दीन्हा ।।

दोहा

करी प्यार ने हू माता, बहुत दिया शिरभार ।
यही जो नीको धारिये, महल द्रव्य सुत नार ।।३९९।।
अब नारी की गति सुनि लीजिए । तामें चित कबहूँ नहिं दीजै ।।
छल बल करि वश अपने राखै । मधुर वचन रसना सों भाखै ।।
कहै कि शिर के छत्र हमारे । हम तौ लागी शरण तुम्हारे ।।
तुम तौ बहुतै लागो पियारे । मोकों तजि मत हूजो न्यारे ।।
ऐसे कहि कहि बांधा चाहै । आठौं अंग काम के बाहै ।।
वस्तर भूषण देह सिंगारै । नाना विधि करि रूप सँवारे ।।
करे कटाक्ष बहुत ही भारै । वश करन को टोना डारै ।।
काजल भरी आँख कूं जोहै । अंग विषे रस दै दै मोहै ।।
ह्यां सूं निकसन कैसे पावै । चरणदास शुकदेव सुनावै ।।

दोहा

में जाल के ही तिरिया, आय फँसै जो कोय ।
तलफि तलफि ह्वाईं रहै, निकसि सके नहिं कोय ।।४००।।
सुत पुत्री वनिता कूँ जानौं । समधान यासूं परिं जानौं ।।
और बँधै बहतै बँदवारा । नाई ब्राह्मण बहु परिवारा ।।
सेढ मशानी देवी भूत । ग्रह नक्षत्रहु लगै अऊत ।।
चौथ अहौई लागै सौन । तिरिया कारण साजौ भौन ।।
औरौ बहुत बखेडै जान । नारी से तोहीं पहिंचान ।।
महा अपरबल दुख तेहिं माहीं । मरिकै चौरासी में जाही ।।
ताते हूजै विगि उदास । समुझि तजौ तिरिया की आस ।।
श्री शुकदेवहि चनणहिं दास । सभी कुटुँब हैं नरक निवासा ।।

दोहा

तोतनी बोली सुतकी, करै चोचवी चाय ।।
मन सोहै बाँधै घनो, छूटन की न उपाय ।।४०१।।
हँसि गोदी में आयकरि, बहुत बढावै नेह ।
तामें घने विकार हैं, अन्तकाल दुख देह ।।४०२।।
मोह लगा मरजाय जब, तन मन लागै आग ।
चरणदास यों कहत हैं, सुख चाहै तो त्याग ।।४०३।।
जिहिं कारण चिन्ता लगै, जबलग घट में प्रान ।
हरि गुरु हिये न आवई, यही जु पूरी हान ।।४०४।।
तन छूटै सुत में रहै, अक न तेरी आस ।
जनम जु शूकर लो लहै, मुये नरकही जास ।।४०५।।
कुटुँब बंध ऐसे करि जानौ । फाँसीगर तिनकूँ पहिँचानौ ।।
तोकूँ डारै नरक मँझारा । ताते हीरिं सबनसे न्यारा ।।
बहुतक दुर्जन हैं घट माहीं । तू उनकूं जानत है नाहीं ।।
है वैरी तू जानत मीता । स्वपनेहूं इनकी नहिं चीता ।।
काम क्रोध अरु लोभहु मोहा । सबही राखैं तासूँ द्रोहा ।।
जिनसे गर्व मछरता मारी । जगत बडाई तिनकी नारी ।।
आपा लिये सदाहीं रहै । टेढे वचन झूँठ बहु कहै ।।
इनके संग घनेही दुष्टी । तेरे तन में रहें अद्दष्टी ।।
नितही करै अकारज तेरा । चरणदास कहैं या विधि घेरा ।।

दोहा

वसे में घट वैरी बहु, तू नहिं जीतत कोय ।
निशिदिन घेरेही रहैं, छुटकारा नहिं होय ।।४०६।।
जो कहुँ निकसी बाहेरै आवै । अरु विरक्तका रूप बनावै ।।
कुटुँब छोडि उपजै वैरागा । जगत रहा चरणों से लागा ।।
कछू वासना मनमें धँसी । जबहीं लोक बडाई हँसी ।।
पुष्ट भयो आपा अभिमान । सहजहि आया मोह दिवान ।।
सबही संगी लिये बुलाय । या विरक्तकूं घेरो आय ।।
ताकूं बांधि मुरंडा कीन्हा । फेरी कुटुम्बके माहीं दीन्हा ।।
कुटुँब मित्र गाढा करि बाँधा । बडी बडी आँडि एसा आंधा ।।

चरणदास कहैं घरमें आया । घटके दुर्जन वाहि बँधाया ।।

दोहा

करि निकसि से में कुनबे, फिर कुनबे में जाय ।

निश्चय नरकी होयगा, दुनिया में दुख पाय ।।४०७।।

एक दृष्टांत एक तपोवन में जा रहा । शीत उष्ण पावस शिर सहा ।।

सूखे पातों किया अहारा । छूटे सबही जग व्यवहारा ।।

रहै ध्यान में निशिदिन लागा । हरि के चरण कमल में पागा ।।

महिमा सुनि राजा तहँ आया । दै परिकरमा शीश नवाया ।।

हाथ जोरि ठाढो फिरि भयो । तपसी मुख ना बैठन कह्यो ।।

ठाढे भये बार बहु भयो । तब राजाने मनमें कही ।।

यह तपसी है बहु अभिमानी । मो आवन महिमा नहिं जानी ।।

ऐसी कहि मन माहीं ऐंठा । आपहि आप भूप वह बैठा ।।

दोहा

रंगे में रंग हरिके जो, भूपन सूं क्या काम ।

चरणदास कुछ भय नहीं, ना कुछ चहिये दाम ।।४०८।।

तपसी कछ्रू न मुख सूं भाषा । राजा उठि चढि मारग लागा ।।

क्रोध भरा महलन में आया । खोटा मन में सता उपाया ।।

पातुरि भेजि वाहि अजमाउँ । भेद झूंठ सांचे को पाऊं ।।

जबहीं पातुरी आज्ञा दीजै । देखि तमाशा वाका लीजै ।।

आयसु लै पातुरी घर आई । प्रथमैं लौंडी एक पठाई ।।

वा तपसी का लावो भेद । कौन वस्तु से वाको हेत ।।

कहाँ सु भोजन करै अहारा । छुटै भजनसूं कौनी बारा ।।

बाँदी गई भाद सो लाई । पातुरि कूं सब बात सुनाई ।।

दोहा

धोयकै मुख जा झारै, फिरि तलावमें न्हाय ।

चरणदास फल पात जो, गिरै पडेही खाय ।।४०९।।

पातुरि सुनि मन में डर पाई । कैसे वाकूं वश करुं जाई ।।

बिन वश किये भूप नहिं रीझै । काढि नगरसूं बहुतै खीझै ।।
ताते मकर पेंच कठु कीजै । तपसी काम नरकमें लीजै ।।
जो कहुँ इच्छा नेकहु पइये । छलबल करिवा मदन जगइये ।।
यह विचारि पातुरि जब कियो । नाना विधि भोजन करि लियो ।।
गई तहां तपसी अस्थाना । वह तौ करत हतो हरि ध्याना ।।
बैठ रही धीरज उर धारी । जबलग उठै ध्यान निरवारी ।।
उठे ध्यानते आँखें खोली । करि दण्डवत नारि यों बोली ।।
पुत्र नहीं हमरे घर माहीं । जिस कारण दर्शनकूं आई ।।
यह कहि भोजन आगे राखा । तपसी भोजन लिया न भाखा ।।
वा दिन तौ योंहि उठि आई । अंगुली टिकन ठौर नहिं पाई ।।
दूजे दिन गइ बहुत सबारा । न्हाकर आये थे उहि बारा ।।
कहा कि भजन हमारा कीजे । हमरे नैनलको सुख दीजै ।।
तपसी कहै न चित्त डोलाऊँ । सूखे पात और फल खाऊँ ।।
पातुरि कहै दूरसूं आई । तुम तौ दयानंत सुखदाई ।।
यही मान मेरो तुम राखो । बहुत नहीं अंगली भरि चाखो ।।
कहि कहि वचन वाहि पघि लाया । अंगुली भरि भोजन चटवाया ।।
चाटत चाटत चाटत रहा । रणजीत कहै यों मन बहि गया ।।

दोहा

करि जोरी कर पातुरिने, बहुरो वचन सुनाय ।
एक बार अरु लीजिये, इन्द्रीजित ऋषिराय ।।४१०।।
फिरि भारी अंगुली भरि लीन्हा । बहरौ मुखके माहीं दीन्हा ।।
अंगुली टिकन काम करि आई । घर आकर बहुतै हुलसाई ।।
फिर ह्वां दिना चार ठहराई । उत नहिं गई यही मन आई ।।
पातुरि चतुर ढीलकूं गई । तपसी कही कहां तुम रही ।।
जबहीं पातुरि प्रीति पिछानी । अपनी कला पैठती जानी ।।
वा दिन व्यंजन कछू न लाई । बहु विधि भोजन बात सुनाई ।।
घर ठाकुर सेवा चित लाऊं । नाना विधि के भोग लगाउं ।।
लै आज्ञा निज भवन पधारी । चरणदास कहै छल कियो नारी ।।

दोहा

किये जीतन कूं तपसी, टेक बाँधि करि वाद ।
हौरै हौरै लायहूं, या जिव्हाके स्वाद ।।४११।।
नाना विधिके स्वाद करि, लै गइ वाही पास ।
कह्यो कि यह परसाद है, लीजै कोई ग्रास ।४१२।।
ठाकुर को परसाद है जु लीजै । याको नाहीं कबहुँ न कीजै ।।
नाहीं किये होय अपराधा । तुम तौ कहिये पूरे साधा ।।
कछूक पातुरि वचन सुनायो । कछूक तपसी के मन आयो ।।
डारो हाथ थारके माहीं । ज्यों ज्यों खात सराहत जाहीं ।।
पातुरि कहो सदा लै आऊं । जो जो ठाकुर भोग लगाऊँ ।।
यामें कछू दोष नहिं लागै । तन मनका सब पातक भागै ।।
वाकूं वश करिकै घर आई । सखियन कूं यह कथा सुनाई ।।
कामदेवकी सौगंध खाऊं। तपसी बँधवा करि दिखलाऊँ ।।

दोहा

रसना स्वादहि वश किये, मनमें जीतन बाद ।
कभी आप बांदी कभी, पहुँचायो परसाद ।।४१३।।
कबहूं वा तपसी ढिग आवै । नाना विधि के भोजन खावै ।।
कबहूं भेजै बांदी हाथा । कहिये छुट्टी मोहिं न नाथा ।।
वह जानै मम सेवा करै । यह तो भजन तपस्या हरै ।।
एक दिना पातुरी ह्वां गई । हाथ जोरि भाषत यों भई ।।
कहों कि भवन पधारो । करौ पवित्तर जूँठनि डारो ।।
लावनकी बहु बात बनाई । सो तपसी के मन नहिं भाई ।।
ह्वांई रही टोना सो कीन्हों । तपसी को मन वश करि लीन्हों ।।
दूजे रसकी कला दिखाई । मोह बडो अरु आँख लजाई ।।
भोर भये फिर बात सुनाई । छलबल करि घरही लै आई ।।
चरणदास तपसी नहिं जानी । अजहूं ठगनी ना पहिंचानी ।।

दोहा

दिया सुख बहु ला घरमें, दिना आठही राखि ।
तपसीहू वा वश भयो, पांचन सूं रस चाखि ।।४१४।।

इन्द्रीवश पातुरी घर आयो । अपने तपका तेज घटाया ।।
सिमटा मन भया फूटकफुटा । लागा ध्यान राम का छूटा ।।
देखौ घरके वैरी किया । पकड बांधि औरै कर दिया ।।
फिरि पातुरी राजा पै गऊ । तपसी ठगन बात सब कही ।।
नेक नेक सब कहि समझाई । तब राजा कूं हाँसी आई ।।
योंहीं कही वेगि लै आवो । वाकी सूरत हमैं दिखाओ ।।
फिरि पातुरि उलटीही धाई । तपसी कूं इक बात सुनाई ।।
राजा दर्शन करन बोनावै । जित सेती खाने कूं आवै ।।
वाकूं चलि करि दरशन दीजै । किरपा प्यार बहुतही कीजै ।।
हम तौ उनकी सदा कहावैं । नित उठि करि मुजरे को जावैं ।।
ह्वां तौ अपना घरही जानौ । उठिये चलिये सकुच न मानौ ।।
पाछे तपसी आगे बाला । ऐसै राजा दुआरे चाला ।।
जा राजा कूं दई अशीशा । राजा बैठे नायो शीशा ।।
हँसकरि कही जु किरपा कीन्हा । यह नगरी अपनी करि लीन्हा ।।
घर बैठे हम दर्शन पाये । वै धनि हैं जो तुमको लाये ।।
तपसी कही धन्य तुम राजा । बहुतन को सारत हौ काजा ।।
तुम्हरो तेज देखि हम चीन्ही । तुमहुँ तपस्या आगे कीन्ही ।।
बिना तपस्या राज न पावै । वेद पुराणन में यों गावै ।।
हमहूं दर्शन तुम्हरे पाये । तपसी कहि यों वचन सुनाये ।।
भूपति बहुत अचम्भा कीन्हा । बहुत द्रव्य पातुरि को दीन्हा ।।
फिर राजा तपसी सूं बोला । खोट हिये का सबरी खोला ।।
एक दिना हम तुम ढिग धाये । वनमें तुम्हरा दर्शन पाये ।।
ठाढ रह्यो हौं बहुती बारा । ना तुम बोले नैन उघारा ।।
आज द्योस ऐसा हद कीन्हा । ह्यांई आ तुम दर्शन दीन्हा ।।
यह सुनि तपसी शोचि विचारा । तबहीं पातुरि सूं भयो न्यारा ।।
वेगहि उठि जंगल कूं गया । चरणदास कहै रमता भया ।।

दोहा

जो इद्रिन के वश भयो, यही हाल ह्वै जाय ।
पछतावा मन में रहै, करै हाय दुख हाय ।।४१५।।
पांचौ चोर महा दुखदाई । सो या जगमें देह फँसाई ।।

तन मन कूं बहु व्याधि लगावैं । कायिक वाचिक पाप चढावैं ।।
करम लगा बहुतै भरमावैं । यमके छप्पन वास दिखावैं ।।
फिर चौरासी माहिं फिरावै । जठर अग्नि में ताहि तपावै ।।
जन्म मरण भारी दुख देवै । मानुष देहका सर्वस लेवै ।।
तीन लोक में डोलै हाला । सुरपुर मृत्य औ पाताला ।।
कैसे मुक्ति धामकूं पावै । जो इंद्रियन के वश हो जावै ।।
छूटै जब गुरु किरपा करैं । चरणदास के शिर कर धरैं ।।

दोहा

स्वारथ केहीं सब सगे, कुटुम्ब मित्र कुल गोत ।
परमारथ समझावई, जो दायलु गुरु होत ।।४१६।।
परमारथ में दुख मिटै, कलह कलपना जाय ।
स्वारथ माहीं सुख नहीं, तामें चित न लगाय ।।४१७।।
स्वारथ में चिन्ता घनी, जो ह्वांकर हो गेह ।
बिना आगकी चिता में, जीवत जारि है देह ।।४१८।।
चिन्ता घट में नागिनी, ताके सुख हैं दोय ।
निशिदिन खाये जात है, जान सकै नहिं कोय ।।४१९।।
ता घट चिन्ता नागिनी, जा मुख जप नहिं होय ।
जो टुक आवै याद भी, उहीं जाय फिरि खोय ।।४२०।।
चिन्ता ही सूं लगत है, चरणदास उर आग ।
तहां ध्यान हरि चरणको, कैसेही अब लाग ।।४२१।।
जगत वासना के विषे, घर चिन्ताका जान ।
जगकी आशा छोडि करि, हरि सुमिरणही ठान ।।४२२।।
आशा नद्दी में चलै, सदा मनोरथ नीर ।
परमारथ उपजै बहै, मन नहिं पकडै धीर ।।४२३।।
धीर विना नहिं ध्यान है, निश्चल जप नहिं होय ।
जो चाहै हरिभक्त कूं, जगत वासना खोय ।।४२४।।
जबलग जग सूं प्रीति है, तब लग दुख अपार ।
भय भारी चिन्ता घनी, भवन पिछानौ दार ।।४२५।।
जगसूं छुटि बाहर परै, उसी समय सब चैन ।
उपजै आनँद परमहीं, तहँ कुछ लेन न दैन ।।४२६।।
रहै एक हरि भक्ति हीं, बाधा सब छुटि जाहिं ।

जबै राम अपनो करैं, वेगहि पकरैं बाहिं ।।४२७।।
तातै सहु मन मेरे मीत । जक्त छुटन की राखो चीत ।।
ऐसा अवसर फिरि नहिं पावै । काहे मानुष देह गँवावै ।।
संगी तेरा नहिं धन धाम । तू क्यों पचै मूढ बेकाम ।।
पिछली गई तासकूं रोय । आगे रही योंहि पत खोय ।।
इक इक घरी अमोलक जान । चेत चेत मत होय अजान ।।
अपने घर का करो सँभाल । ललकारत आवत है काल ।।
यातै कीजै यही विचार । डारि सिदौसी जम जंजार ।।
शुकदेव कहैं सुन चरणदासहिं दास । हरि के चरण कमल कर वास ।।

दोहा
कीजिये न ढील यामें, यह विचार मन आन ।
चरणदास यों कहत है, यह गोयह मैदान ।।४२८।।
आयुर्दा यों जात है, ज्यों तरुवर की छांह ।
चेतसि तावी भक्ति में, तजो जगत की बाह ।।४२९।।
तूही पकरो जगत ने, तैंहीं पकरो आय ।
ज्यों नलिनी को सूवटा, धोखे पकडो जाय ।।४३०।।
जैसे बांदर आपहि फँसिया । समझवान मन माहीं हँसिया ।।
मूठ चनों की जो वह तजता । तौ काहे कूं फँसा जु रहता ।।
ज्यों कांटे सूं मच्छी लागी । आपहिं आई चली अभागी ।।
सरुवर में तरुवर की छांहीं । अजया देखि गिरी वा माहीं ।।
जैसे पक्षी जाल मँझारा । आपहि आय फँसा बज मारा ।।
खन्कद में हाथी आ परिया । लेन गयो कोउ आपहि गिरिया ।।
बाजत बीण मृगा चलि आया । पकर कौन चंचल कूं ल्याया ।।
योंहीं तुम अपनी गति जानौ । आपहिं बँधे यही पहिंचानौ ।।
ऐसे जगत तोहिं नहिं पकडा । चरणदास कहैं योंहीं जकडा ।।

दोहा
जगत छोड की वासना, यही जु छूटन उपाव ।
ये मन ऐसी धारिये, अबहीं नीको दांव ।।४३१।।
अबकी चूके चूक है, फिर पछितावा होय ।

जो तुम जक्त न छांहिहौ, जन्म जायगो खाय ।।४३२।।
जग माहीं न्यारे रहो, लगे रहो हरि ध्यान।
पृथ्वी पर देही रहै, परमेश्वर में प्राण ।।४३३।।
ज्यों तिरिया पीहर बसै, सुरति पिया के माहिं ।
ऐसे जन जग में रहैं, हरि कूं भूलै नाहिं ।।४३४।।
ज्यों किरपण बहु दामहीं, गाडि जिमीके नीच ।
सदा वाही तकतो रहै, सुरति रहै ता बीच ।।४३५।।
तन छूटै हो सरपही, जा बैठे वा ठौर ।
जहां आशा तहँ वास है, कहूं न भर्मै और ।।४३६।।
चित रहै गोविंद के विषे, जग में सहज सुभाय ।
तन छूटै हरि कूं मिलै, चरणकमल लपटाय ।।४३७।।
जग त्यागो वैराग लै, निश्चय मन कूं लाव ।
आठ पहर साठौ घरी, सुमिरन सुरति लगाव ।।४३८।।
सब सूं रहु निरवैरता, गहौ दीनता ध्यान ।
अन्त मूक्ति पद पाइहौ, जग में होय न हान ।।४३९।।
चरणदास यों कहत हैं, बडी दीनता जान ।
औरन की तौ क्या चलै, लगै न माया बान ।।४४०।।
दया नम्रता दीनता, क्षमा शील संतोष ।
इनकूं लै सुमिरण करै, निश्चय पावै मौष ।।४४१।।
ये सब लक्षण राम में, प्रगटत देखैं मोहिं ।
जो वे आवैं तुझ विषे, प्यार करैं हरि तोहिं ।।४४२।।
हरि सूं प्रीति लगाय कै, सबनों लेहि उठाय ।
रहै सदा इक राम हीं, और सकल मिट जाय ।।४४३।।
मिटते सूं प्रीति मत कर, रहते सूं कर नेह ।
झूठे कूं तजि दीजिये, सांच में करि गेह ।।४४४।।
सांचा हरि का नाम है, झूठा यह संसार ।
शुकदेव कहै चरणदास हो, सुमिरण करौ विचार ।।४४५।।
दश इंद्रिन कूं खैंच करि, अभय अमर फल चाख ।
सहजहि सुमिरण होत है, तामें मन कूं राख ।।४४६।।
मानसरोवर देह में, मुक्ताहल जो स्वाँस ।
चुगिये हंस स्वरूप ह्वै, खुलै कर्म्म की गांस ।।४४७।।
अजपा को यहि अर्थ है, बिना जपेही होत ।

कछुवा की ज्यों सिमट करि, तहां लगावो गोत ॥४४८॥
आवतहीं कूं देखिये, जाते कूं जो निहारि ।
ऐसे सुरत लगाइये, चरणदास हिय धारि ॥४४९॥
सक्कारे तन सींचिये, हक्कारे सुख होय ।
ऐसे सुमिरण सत्त कूँ, जानै बिरला कोय ॥४५०॥
नाभिहि सेती उठत है, फिरि तामाहिं समाय ।
याको भेद अपार है, सद्गुरु देहि बताय ॥४५१॥
नाभि नासिका माहिं करि, घाल हिंडोला झूल ।
उपजै अति आनन्दही, रहै न दुख का मूल ॥४५२॥
ब्रह्म सिंधु की लहर है, तामें न्हान सजोय ।
कलिमल सब छुटि जायँगे, पातक रहे न कोय ॥४५३॥
अरसठ तीरथ तो विषे, बाहर क्यों भटकाव ।
चरणदास यों कहत है, उलटाही घर आव ॥४५४॥
श्वासा सँभल विचारि करि, तहां करो विश्राम ।
जाते हरि ही हरि कहौ, आवत कहिये श्याम ॥४५५॥
श्वासा लेवै नाम बिन, सो जीवन धिक्कार ।
श्वास श्वास में राम जप, यही धारणा धार ॥४५६॥
उलट पलट जप रामहीं, टेढा सीधा होय ।
याका फल नहिं जायगा, कैसे ही लोकोय ॥४५७॥
खाते पाते नाम ले, बैठे चलते सोय ।
सदा पवित्तर नाम है, करै ऊजला तोय ॥४५८॥
नीचन कू उँचा करै, ऊंचन को कर देव ।
देवन कूं हरि ही करै, रहै न दूजा भेव ॥४५९॥
भरमत भरमत आइया, पाई मावुष देह ।
ऐसो अवसर फिरि कहां, नाम शिताबी लेह ॥४६०॥
कै घर में कै बाहरे, जो चित आवै नाम ।
दोनों होहिं बराबरी, कै जंगल कै ग्राम ॥४६१॥
करै तपस्या नाम बिन, योग यज्ञ अरु दान ।
चरणदास यों कहत हैं, सबही थोथे जान ॥४६२॥
अधिकी ऊंचा नाम है, सब करणी का जीव ।
अष्टादश अरु चारिका, मथि करि काढा घीव ॥४६३॥
चारों युग में द्खि ले, जिन जपिया जिन नाव ।

टेक पकरि आगे धँसे, परा न पीछे पाव ।।४६४।।
जैसी गति उनकी भई, गावत साधु पुरान ।
वैसी तेरी होयगी, यह निश्चय करि जान ।।४६५।।
दुख धन्धे कूं छोडि करि, कलह कल्पना त्याग ।
शुकदेव कहि चरणदास कूं, राम भजन में लाग ।।४६६।।
हरि के गुण माला करौ, रसना ऊपर लाव ।
किया किया ही देखि करि, ताहि सराहत जाव ।।४६७।।
देखि देखि देख रहो, अस्तुति मुख सूं भाख।
वाकी चतुराई सबै, ले करि मन में राख ।।४६८।।
वैसा तो रँगरेज ना, वैसे छीपी नाहिं ।
वैसा कारीगर नहीं, या दुनिया माहिं ।।४६९।।
अजब अजब अचरज किये, अद्‌भुत अधिक अपार ।
जल थल पवन अकाश में, देखो दृष्टि अधार ।।४७०।।
सृष्टि बाग माली रचौ, भाँति भाँति गुलजार ।
रीझ रीझ शिर दीजिये, एहो निरख बहार ।।४७१।।
कबहूं जग परगट करै, कबहूं करै अलोप ।
नाना विधि बाजी करै, आप रहत है गोप ।।४७२।।
बाजीगर बाजी रची, सब गति पूरण साज ।
किये तमाशे बहुतही, तोहिं दिखावन काज ।।४७३।।
देखी होय परसन्नहीं, तू वाको गुण मान ।
चरणदास जो बुद्धि है, अधिक सुघरता जान ।।४७४।।
बहुत प्यार तो पे करैं, तू नहिं जानत सार ।
वाहि भुला यों हीं रहै, नेक न करैं सँभार ।।४७५।।
राम बिसारो आदि सूं, लियो द्रव्य अरु नार ।
याही ते भरमत फिरो, तन धरि वारंवार ।।४७६।।
गई सु गइ अब राखि ले, एहो मूढ अयान ।
निष्केवल हरि कूं रटौ, सीख गुरु की मान ।।४७७।।
सोवन में नहिं खोइये, जन्म पदारथ पाय ।
चरणदास ह्वै जागिये, आलस सकल गँवाय ।।४७८।।
सोवन ही में हानि है, जागन में बहु लाभ ।
बुद्धि उज्ज्वल ही होत है, मुख पर चढै जु आभ ।।४७९।।
दिनकूं हरि सुमिरण करौ, रैनि जाग करि ध्यान ।

भूँख राखि भोजन करौ, तजि सोवन की बान ।।४८०।।
चारि पहर नहिं जगि सकै, आधी रात सु जाग ।
ध्यान करो जप ही करी, भजन करन कूं लाग ।।४८१।।
जो नहिं श्रद्धा दो पहर, पिछले पहर चेत ।
उठ बैठे रटना रटै, प्रभु सूं लावहि हेत ।।४८२।।
जागै ना पिछिले पहर, ताते मुखडे धूल ।
सुमिरे ना करतार कूं, सभी गँवावै मूल ।।४८३।।
जागै ना पिछिलै पहर, कहै ना आतमध्यान ।
ते नर नरकै जाइँगे, बहुत सहैं यमसान ।।४८४।।
जागै ना पिछिलै पहर, करे न गुरु मत जाप ।
मुँह फारे सोवत रहै, ताको लागै पाप ।।४८५।।
पिछिलै पहर जागि करि, भजन करै चितलाय ।
चरणदास वा जीव की, निश्चय गति ह्वै जाय ।।४८६।।
पिछिलै पहर जागि करि, भरि भरि अमृत पीव ।
विषय जक्त ना रहै, अमर होय करि जीव ।।४८७।।
जन्म छूटै मरणा छूटै, आवागमन छुटि जाय ।
एक पहर की रात सूं, बैठा हौ गुण गाय ।।४८८।।
पहिले पहरे सब जगै, दूजे भोगी मान ।
तीजे पहरे चोर ही, चौथे योगी जान ।।४८९।।
मरयादा की यह कही, क्या विरक्त परमान ।
आठै पहर साठा घरी, जागे हरि के ध्यान ।।४९०।।
जे कोइ विरही राम के, तिनकूं कैसी नींद ।
शस्तर लागा नेह का, गया हिये को बींद ।।४९१।।
तिनसे जग सहजै छुटा, कहां रंग कहँ भूप ।
चले गये घर छोंडिके, धरि विरक्त का रूप ।।४९२।।
जिनको मन बिरकत सदा, रहौ जहाँ चित होय ।
घर बाहर दोउ एकसा, जारी दुविधा खोय ।।४९३।।
सोये हैं संसार सूं, जागे हरि की ओर ।
तिनकूं इक रसही सदा, नहीं साँझ नहिं भौर ।।४९४।।
उनकूं नींद न आवई, राम मिलन की चीत ।
सोवै ना सुख सेज है, तजि कै हरि सों मीत ।।४९५।।
कैसे वै हरि सूं मिले, जिनके ऊंचे भाग ।

कैसे व हरि त्यागि कै, रहे जगत सूं लाग ।।४९६।।
सोवन जागन भेद की, कोइक जानत बात ।
साधू जन जागत तहां, जहां सबन की रात ।।४९७।।
जो जागै हरि भक्ति में, सोई उतरै पार ।
जो जागै संसार में, भवसागर में ख्वार ।।४९८।।
कै जागत हूका भरा, कै जागा वश काम ।
कै जागा जग टहल में, लाग रहौ धन धाम ।।४९९।।
ऐसे जन्म गँवाय दिया, महा मूढ अज्ञान ।
चौरासी में फिरि चलै, मन का कहा जु मान ।।५००।।
सद्गुरु शरणै आयकरि, कहा ना मानै एक ।
ते नर बहु दुख पाइहैं, तिनकूं सुख नहिं नेक ।।५०१।।
सद्गुरु चरणौ ना लगे, किया न हरि का खोज ।
सो खर कूकर शूकरा, अरु जंगल का रोझ ।।५०१।।
पेट भरे भर सोइया, ते नर पशू समान ।
परनारी कै आपनी, तिनको नाहीं ज्ञान ।।५०३।।
जैसा तैसा खाय करि, पेट भरे भरि लेह ।
पडकर सोवै भोर लों, सो शूकर की देह ।।५०४।।
हरि चरचा बिन जो बकै, सो कूकर की भूत ।
कह रणजित वह साँझला, खाय धूस ही धूस ।।५०५।।
जो पावै सोई चरै, करै नहीं पहिंचान ।
पीठ लदै हरि ना जपै, ताकूं खरही जान ।।५०६।।
रोझ जान वा देह कूं, ताकूं नहीं विचार ।
फिरै बिना मर्य्यादही, बताहु करै अहार ।।५०७।।
बहुता किये अहार ही, मैली रहै जु बुद्धि ।
हरि के निर्मल नाम की, कैसे आवै शुद्धि ।।५०८।।
सूक्षम भोजन खाइ करि, रहिये ना परि सोय ।
ऐसी मानुष देह कूं, भक्ति बिना मत खोय ।।५०९।।
जन्म चलोही जात है, ज्यों कूवै में लाव ।
दौरत मृग की छाँव को, नेक नहीं ठहराव ।।५१०।।
समझ शिताबी भक्ति ले, नेक न ढील लगाव ।
आपा हरि कूं दे चुको, योको यही उपाव ।।५११।।
जग का कहा न मानिये, सद्गुरु सो लै बुद्धि ।

ताकूं हिय में राखिये, करो शिताबी शुद्धि ।।५१२।।
गुरु सेती सद्गुरु बडे, परमेश्वर के रूप ।
मक्ति छांह पहुँचाय दें, जगत छुटावै धूप ।।५१३।।
कु.पहिला कहू दाई गुरु, दूजे माई जान ।
तीजा गुरु खिलावडी, चौथा पिता पिछान ।।
पांचवें पाधा जानौ । कनफूका गुरु छठा, तास पूजा दे मानौ ।।
सतवां सद्गुरु जानिये, जग सूं करैं उदास ।
मुक्ति धाम सोइ देत हैं, कहैं चरणहि दास ।।

दोहा
कहै ऐसे मिलते गुरु, कछू लाय मोहिं देह ।
सद्गुरु मिल ऐसे कहै, नाम धनी का लेह ।।५१४।।
कनफूका गुरु जगत का, राम मिलावन और ।
सो सद्गुरु को जानिये, मुक्ति दिखावन ठौर ।।५१५।।
गलियारे गुरु फिरत हैं, घर घर कंठी देत ।
और काज उनकूं नहीं, द्रव्य कमावन हेत ।।५१६।।
सद्गुरु डंका देत हैं, भक्ति राम की लेहु ।
पहिले हमकूं भेंटही, शीश आपनो देहु ।।५१७।।
सो सद्गुरु शुकदेव हैं, समझि हिये में राखि ।
तिनके शरणै आव मन, चरणदास कहे भाखि ।।५१८।।
यग सिगरो उपदेश ही, मैं आपन कूं दीन ।
मो मन कूं आपा घना, कहीं होय आधीन ।।५१९।।
सद्गुरु सूं मांगौ यही, मोहि गरीबी देहु ।
दूर बडप्पन कीजिये, नान्हा ही करि लेहु ।।५२०।।
जनक परम गुरु देवजी, सुनु सद्गुरु शुकदेव ।
यही अर्ज मैं करत हूं, मोहि साधु करि लेव ।।५२१।।
चारों युग के भक्त जन, तुम हौ सुख के धाम ।
चरणहिंदासा होय कै, तुम्हें करूं परणाम ।।५२२।।
आदि पुरुष किरपा करौ, सब अवगुण छुटि जाहिं ।
साध होन लक्षण मिलैं, चरणकमल की छाहिं ।।५२३।।
तुम्हरी शक्ति अपार है, लीला को नहिं अन्त ।
चरणदास यों कहत हैं, ऐसे तुम भगवन्त ।।५२४।।

छप्पय

रूप जगत में आप रच्यो, नारायण कीन्हों।
दूजे लक्ष्मी भई बहुरी, पानी रँग भीन्हों।।
नाभिकमल फिरि भयो, जहां ब्रह्माजी उपजे।
विधि की त्रिकुटी माहिं, तहां शंकरजी निपजे।।
चारि वेद अरु विष्णु ह्वै, सकल जगत छिन में कियो।
निराकार आकार सों, चरणदाम जिहिं मन दियो।।

कवित्त

राम अडिग्ग तो वही, चौथे पद वास जाको,
वही तौ अडिग्ग राम मथुरा में आयो है।
वही तौ अडिग्ग राम योगी जाका ध्यान धरै,
वही तौ अडिग्ग राम सीता पति पायो है।।
वही तौ अडिग्ग राम सभी ठाम रमि रह्यो,
वही तौ अडिग्ग राम संतन सहायो है।
वही तौ अडिग्ग राम चरणदास चेरो जाको,
वही तौ अडिग्ग राम काया खोजी पायो है।।
माया भ्रम फंद देख साधन को संग पेख,
राम को पहिरि भेख कंचन तन ताव रे।
मन कूं पहिंचान ज्ञान एकाएकी सबै जान,
नाद के गहेते तू अनहद बजाव रे।।
उलटि पलटि काया बीच चारों कर दूर,
ऐसी विधि मेरु पै समीर कूं चढाव रे।
कहैं चरणदास गगन मध्य करो वास,
जहां नहीं शीत उष्ण निर्भय पद ध्याव रे।।

दोहा

गये रावण दुर्योधन, अरु यादव परिवार।
चरणदास थिर कोइ नहीं, होय मिटै संसार।।५२६।।

कवित्त

जाव बिहानो सो भोर, ढेरैगी दुपहरीसी, समझ विचारि देखि चली आवे रात है।

भँवत सुचान काल तेरे पर तकि रहो, छिन पलकी खब्र नाहिं करे आय घात है ।।
दारा सुत द्रव्य सब सपन को सुख भयो, जानहुगे जभी जब छूटि जाय जात है ।
कहै चरणदास अब तजै क्यों न विषय वास, पानी माहिं नाव जैसे आयु चली जात है ।।

कुमार सूं भाज और लाज खोटे करमन सूं, चौरासी के त्राम सूं मूढ क्यों न लज रे ।
साधुन के संग बैठि धमहू की नाव लेटि, गुरुहू को ज्ञान राखि प्रेम भक्ति सज रे ।।
छूटे जब नारी यम देवै दुख भारी डारैं, नरक मँझारी आवागमन क्यों न तज रे ।
कहै चरणदास तजे क्यों न विषय वास, राम के सँवारे अब राम रास भज रे।।

सवैया

वश जडता में जग रहो भूलि, दारा सुता सुत प्रीति बढावै ।
इन सूं मन बाँटि रहो गृह बीच सो, अन्त समैं कोइ पास न जावै ।।
आनि गहै यमजाम तेरो सबही, मिलि प्रीतम राम बतावै ।
चरणदास कहै चेतौ नर मूरख, राम बिना कोइ काम न आवै ।।

कवित्त

कूं देवन भस्म धावै, भीतन के लेवन को कोई संग साथी नाहिं भीर परे तेरा है ।
परसता है चण्डकी भूत अरु शीतला कूं, भजै क्यों न रामनाम कटै यम बेरा है ।।
भैरौं अरु बराही पाखंड पूजा सभी करै, है सब हरि किन्हूं नैनन न हेरा है ।।
चरणदास कूर सब सन्तन को चेरो कहैं, ऐसा जग अन्धा जानि कर्मनने घेरा है ।।

दोहा

हलावन मूंड टोना यंतर, और कीसियाँ झूठ ।
चरणदास कहैं सब भगल है, यह जग लीन्हा लूट ।।५२६।।

कवित्त

सेवे भूतन, तो भूतन में जाय मिलै, जादू को सेवै सो चमार ताकी माई सूं।
देवतों कूं सेवै तौ देवलोक बास लहै, औषधी कूं सेवै तौ मिलाप रावराई सूं ।
कीमियां सेवै तौ खराब होय दुनिया में, ऐसे धन खोवै जो सुनावै नहीं भाई सूं ।
कहै चरणदास हम इतने कूं मानै नाहिं,
देखी सबी छांडि मान लगो है कन्हाई सूं।।

कु. पारा ना मारा मरे गंधक होय न तेल ।
केते पचि पचि मरि गये, शिर में मिट्टी मेल ।।
शिर में मिट्टी मेल भटक करि जन्म सिरायो ।
जडी बूटि कूं फिरै कहीं, कुछ हाथ ना आयो ।।
बौरे हरि क्यों न भजै, काहे जन्म सिरायो ।
चरणदास कीमियां झूठो, गुरु शुकदेव सुनायो ।।
अरिल्ल सेवत पाँचकी सात, जो लगि एक सूं ।
साधन की करि सेव मुँडो मत भेष कूं ।।
भेषी माहिं अलेख यही तू जानियो ।
चरणदास की सीख निश्चय करि मानियो ।।

दोहा
नहीं करै भजन आपै, औरे मने करैं ।
चरणदास कहैं व दुष्ट नर, भर्म भर्म नरकै परैं ।।५२७।।
औरन कूं उपदेश करि, भजन करैं निष्काम ।
चरणदास वे साधुजन, पहुँचै हरि के धाम ।।५२८।।
शून्य शहर हम बसत हैं, अनहद है कुलदेव ।
अजपा गोत विचारि ले, चरणदास यहि भेव ।।५२९।।
भक्ति पदारथ उदय सूं, होय सभी कल्याण ।
पढैं सुनैं सेवन करैं, पावै पद निर्वान ।।५३०।।
भक्ति पदारथ मैं कही, कछु इक भेद बखान ।
जो कोइ समझै प्रीति सूं, छूटै यमदुख सान ।।५३१।।
पाठ करै मन में धरै, बहुरूं करै विचार ।
कहै गुरु शुकदेवजी, उतरै भवजल पार ।।५३२।।
जय जय श्री शुकदेवजी, तुम्हैं करूं परणाम ।
तुम प्रसाद पोथी कही, भये जो पूरण काम ।।५३३।।
हिरदय में शीतल हुये, तपनि गी सब दूर ।
या बाणी के कहेते, कायर मन भयो शूर ।।५३४।।
चन्दन चरचै पुष्प धरि, बहुरी करै परणाम ।
कथा बांचि सबही सुनै, कहा पुरुष कह वाम ।।५३५।।
कहै सुनै जो प्रेम सूं, वाकूं राखै याद ।
चरणदास यो कहत हैं, बनि हौ पूरे साध ।।५३६।।

Bibliography

Aveling, H., & Friedlander, P. (2005). *The Songs of Daya Bai: Daya Bai Ki Bani*. New Delhi: Prestige Books.

Aveling, H., & Joshi, S. (2001). *Sahaj Prakash: The Brightness of Simplicity*. New Delhi: Motilal Banarasidass.

Bahurā, G.N. (1982). *The Padas of Surdas*. Jaipur: Maharaja Sawaii Singh Museum Trust.

Blumhardt, J.F. (1893). *Catalogues of the Hindi Panjabi Sindhi and Pushtu Printed Books*. London: Kegan Paul Trench, Trubner.

Blumhardt, J.F. (1913). *A Supplementary Catalogue of Hindi Books in the Library of the British Museum acquired during the Years 1893-1912*. London: British Museum.

Callewaert, W.M., & Friedlander, P. (1992). *The Life and Works of Raidas*. New Delhi: Manohar.

Caraṇdās (1903). *Śrīsvāmī Caraṇdāsjī ke Granth*. Lakhnaū: Avadha Samācar Patra.

Caraṇdās (1908). *Caraṇdās kī Bāṇī*. Ilāhābāda: Belaveḍiyar Ṣṭīm Priṇtiṅg Varks.

Caraṇdās (1999). *Śrī Bhakti Sāgar*. Jaypur: Śrī Saras Nikuñj.

Caraṇdās (2001). *Bhaktisāgarādi*. Mumbaī: Khemrāj Śrīkṛṣṇadās Prakāśan.

Caturvedī, K.K. (1992). *Bhakti Sāgar kā Pāṭh-Sampādan*. Allahabad: Raka Prakāśan.

Caturvedī, P. (1966). *Dādū Granthāvalī*. Vārāṇasī: Nāgarī Pracāranī Sābha.

Caturvedī, P. (1972). *Uttarī Bhārat kī Sant Paramparā*. Ilāhābād: Bhārtī Bhaṇḍār.

Crooke, W. (1896). *The Tribes and Castes of the North-West Provinces and Oudh*. Calcutta: Office of the Superintendent of Government Printing.

Dās, G. (2000). *Śrī Śyām Caraṇ Dās jī kā saṅkṣipt Jīvan Caritra*. Dillī: Gaddī Suśrī Sahajo Bāī jī.

Dharmdās. (1985). *Dhanī Dharamdās kī Śabdāvalī* Ilāhābād: Belvīdiyar Priṇṭiṅg Varks.

Dvivedī, G. (1974). *Hindī santkāvya sangrah*. Ilāhābād: Hindustānī Ekeḍemī.

Friedlander, P. (1996). *A Descriptive Catalogue of the Hindi Manuscripts in the Library of the Wellcome Institute*. London: The Wellcome Institute for the History of Medicine.

Gaṅgādās (1968). *Śrī Śyām Caraṇ Dās Caritāvalī. Dehlī: Śrī Śyām Caraṇ Dās Prakaśan Kāryālay.*

Gold, D. (1987). *The Lord as Guru: Hindi Sants in the Northern Indian Tradition*. New York: Oxford University Press.

_____. (1992). What the Merchant-Guru Sold: Social and Literary Types in Hindi Devotional Verse. *Journal of the American Oriental Society*, 112(1), 22-35.

Grierson, G.A. (1910). Charan Dāsīs. In J. Hasting, ed., *Encyclopedia of Religion and Ethics* (Vol. 3, pp. 365-368). Edinburgh: T & T Clark.

Jurgensmeyer, M. (1995). The Social Significance of Radhasoami. In D. Lorenzen, ed., *Bhakti Religion in North India* (pp. 67-93). Albany, NY: State University of New York Press.

Kabīr (1989a). *Kabīr Sāheb Kī Śabdāvalī Pahalā Bhāg*. Ilāhābād: Belvīḍiyar Priṇṭing Varks.

Kabīr (1989b). *Kabīr Sāheb Kī Śabdāvalī Dūsrā Bhāg*. Ilāhābād: Belvīḍiyar Priṇṭing Varks.

Keay, F.E. (1920). *A History of Hindi Literature*. Calcutta: Association Press.

McGregor, R.S. (1984). *Hindi literature of the nineteenth and early twentieth centuries* (Vol. 8, Part 1). Verlag: Otto Harrassowitz.

Rajneesh, Osho (2001). *The Last Morning Star*, trans. Harry Aveling (Swami Anand Haridas) and Sudha Joshi. Pune: Rebel.

Rajnīś, Bhagvān Śrī (1978). *Nahīṃ sāñjha nahīm bhor*. Pūne: Rajnīś Fāuṇḍeśan.

Rose, H.A. (1911). *A Glossary of the Tribes and Castes of the Punjab and North-West Frontier Province* (Vol. II). Lahore: Civil and Military Gazette.

Śarmā, B.P. (1978). *Nānak Vāṇī*. Canḍigaṛh: Viśva Bhārati Prakāśan.

Schomer, K. & McLeod, W.H., ed. (1987). *The Sants*, Delhi: Motilal Banarasidass

Starke, U. (2007). *An Empire of Books*. New Delhi: Permanent Black.

Śukla, Ś. (1995). *Caraṇdāsī Sampradāy aur uskā Sāhitya*. Vārāṇasī: Kalā Prakāśan.

Tiwari, O.P. (1983). *Astanga Yoga of Saint Charandas*. Lonavla: Kaivalyadhama.

Vaudeville, C. (1974). *Kabīr*. Oxford: Oxford University Press.

Wilson, H.H. (1904). *Essays and Lectures on the Religions of the Hindus*. London: Trübner.